The Educated Woman in America

SELECTED WRITINGS OF CATHARINE BEECHER, MARGARET FULLER, AND M. CAREY THOMAS

Edited, with an Introduction and Notes, by

BARBARA M. CROSS

☆

CLASSICS IN

No. 25

EDUCATION

☆

TEACHERS COLLEGE PRESS
TEACHERS COLLEGE, COLUMBIA UNIVERSITY
NEW YORK

Library of Congress Catalog Card
Number 65-23578

Second Printing, 1974

Printed in the United States of America

Preface

"In no country has such constant care been taken as in America to trace two clearly distinct lines of action for the two sexes and to make them keep pace one with the other, but in two pathways that are always different." Thus did the perceptive young Tocqueville characterize the relationship between the sexes in his classic treatise, *Democracy in America* (1835). Here as elsewhere in the new society, he saw the principle of equality working its prodigious influence on ideas, habits, and institutions. But it was an equality of condition, not of office, he hastened to point out. Women took no part in business or in politics; they never managed "the outward concerns of the family." With rare exceptions they were confined to "the quiet circle of domestic employments." Americans had simply applied to the sexes "the great principle of political economy which governs the manufacturers of our age, by carefully dividing the duties of man from those of woman in order that the great work of society may be the better carried on."

A half-century later, when the equally perceptive James Bryce wrote *The American Commonwealth* (1888), it was apparent that a revolution had been wrought. Bryce reported that American women had achieved genuine equality of private rights; that they had gained access to virtually all the professions—certainly to medicine, law, the ministry, teaching, journalism, business, and politics; and, indeed, that they had won sufficient opportunity for advanced education to occasion widespread complaints that girls of the humbler classes were being raised out of the sphere to which their means would destine them. "Taking one thing with another," Bryce estimated, "it is easier for women to find a career, to obtain remunerative work of an intellectual as of a commercial or mechanical kind, than in any part of Europe." The result he perceived as a "new type of womanhood," which was already exerting a profoundly wholesome effect on American society at large.

Professor Cross's volume deals with one fundamental aspect of this revolution in the relationship between the sexes—the design of a new "archetype of ideal femininity." Catharine Beecher, Margaret Fuller, and M. Carey Thomas were in the vanguard of those "new women" who, by insistent preachment and radical educational innovation, literally transformed the American character. They were often graceless, occasionally tiresome, and almost always irritating, but the very nature of their lives educated the American people. And as Mrs. Cross concludes, they added immeasurably to the live options of present-day women "by making the feminine' seem legitimately various."

Those who would delve further into the fascinating educational problems raised by the documents that follow and by Mrs. Cross's commentary on them might turn with profit to Thomas Woody, *A History of Women's Education in the United States* (1929), and Mabel Newcomer, *A Century of Higher Education for American Women* (1959).

LAWRENCE A. CREMIN

Contents

The Educated Woman
in America

SELECTED WRITINGS OF
CATHARINE BEECHER,
MARGARET FULLER,
AND M. CAREY THOMAS

Introduction

By BARBARA M. CROSS

David Potter has recently pointed out that historians and sociologists generalizing about "the American character" have based their analyses on the American man. Their neglect of the other sex is curious, for from the time of Hawthorne's Hester Prynne through the creation of Henry Adams' Virgin and Henry James's Milly Theale, American men celebrated the strange powers of women; and American women themselves have long constituted an articulate and self-conscious crew. Though Puritan writers assumed that the daughters of Eve shared her concupiscence, weakness, and unfortunate persuasiveness, in colonial America the mere shortage of women helped inflate their value. By the early nineteenth century, when the emigration of men westward had left a surplus of women in the East, a tradition of respect had been established; and Catharine Beecher, writing from the 1830's through the 1860's, assumed that the American woman had onerous and peculiar duties, which derived largely from the crudeness and disorder of an expanding nation. So she urged girls to head west, since as teachers and wives they could recreate in the wilderness the high-minded domesticity of the East. After Miss Beecher's time, the American woman continued to be seen as the peculiar custodian of spiritual things; and in the early twentieth century, M. Carey Thomas, briskly noting the

1

boorish materialism of the "captains of industry," urged Bryn Mawr students to preserve the cultural inheritance embodied in a liberal arts education.[1]

Between the 1830's, when Catharine Beecher started her crusade, and the 1930's, when M. Carey Thomas finished hers, American men and women tried persistently to design an archetype of ideal femininity. Unlike the satire of a Jean de Meun or an Alexander Pope, and unlike the cautious realism of a Cotton Mather, exuberant eulogy eventually became the keynote of the American writers' analyses. But though writers agreed to praise, the question of what was good about women remained ticklish and controversial, as the selections in this volume reveal.[2]

Still, the years of agitation fashioned the "new woman," whom Henry Adams glumly assessed at the opening of the twentieth century. "All these new women," he noted, "had been created since 1840; all were to show their meaning before 1940." The writings of Catharine Beecher, Margaret Fuller, and M. Carey Thomas helped shape this new creature, "sexless as the bees," with "nothing to rebel against except her own maternity," just as their pioneering certainties help explain Adams' ambivalence toward the sex that had moved from centripetal Virgin to modern woman, "free and volatized like

[1] David Potter, "American Women and the American Character," in *American Character and Culture*, edited by John A. Hague (Deland, Fla., 1964), pp. 65–85; Levin L. Schücking, *Die Familie im Puritanismus* (Leipzig, 1929), Chap. 1; see M. Carey Thomas, Addresses to the Bryn Mawr undergraduates, 1900–1912 (Bryn Mawr College Archives).

[2] See Cotton Mather, *Ornaments for the Daughters of Zion* (Boston, 1962), p. 30: "The Happiness of a Virtuous Woman is that she shall be Praised. Praise, Reputation, Commemoration is that which a Woman is very tender of." Catharine Beecher would never have admitted such worldly motives in her virtuous housewives.

Clerk Maxwell's perfect gas." For, like Adams, they had lived with visions of the truly feminine, visions that made them snappish and devout.[3]

In many ways they were difficult: loud, peculiar, and exacting. They were spinsters conscious of being chosen among women, worriers about the "woman question," who deplored the roles of belle and society matron in which many of their sex uncritically thrived. They set out to redefine "the feminine," and they largely succeeded in their presumptuous task. For the very irritability of their hopes spoke to their sex and to their nation. They lived in times of protest and revolt; the century and a half between the birth of Catharine Beecher and the death of M. Carey Thomas issued in the enfranchised woman, who could vote and practice law or medicine, who could be a "Bloomer girl" or a flapper or, if she were lucky, have "IT," yet who in the end still complained. In 1848, when Catharine Beecher was forty-eight and Margaret Fuller thirty-eight, the Seneca Falls Convention on Woman's Rights resolved that "the history of mankind is a history of repeated injuries and usurpations on the part of man toward woman"; and in 1883, one year after M. Carey Thomas received her Ph.D., Henry James, searching for a peculiarly "American" subject, hit upon women, "the agitation on their behalf" and the failure of "the sentiment of sex."[4]

II

Catharine Beecher was the most conservative of the three. The oldest and favorite child in a family of thir-

3 *The Education of Henry Adams* (Boston, 1918), pp. 441–446.
4 *The Notebooks of Henry James,* edited by F. O. Matthiessen and Kenneth B. Murdock (New York, 1947), p. 47.

teen, she enjoyed the publicity and importance accorded
a minister's daughter. During her childhood, she saw her
father, Lyman Beecher, become famous as a revivalist and
preacher. His "constant companion," she considered him
her "playmate" and counted on his indulgence. She was
poetess and dramatist for the family; her role was to
make them laugh and to show her pluckiness when her
father swung her out of an attic window or suddenly
pushed her head into a basin of water. The Litchfield
school she attended did not count for much in the nervous, frisky household, where Lyman Beecher frolicked,
fiddled, danced in his stocking feet, and won souls for the
gospel; where his beloved wife Roxanne painted flam-
boyant flowers on her carpet, read Maria Edgeworth, Sir
Walter Scott, and *The Christian Observer*, and was
adored as the sole example of "disinterested benevolence" her husband had ever known; and where Catharine "did little else but play." As Catharine grew older,
she and her mother shared her father's "elevated
thoughts" on the unique Edwardsian virtue of benevolence and on the duties of temperance, Bible reading,
conversion, and missions. If she was not pretty, she impressed the family with her cocky wit and compelled ad-
miration even if she did not always inspire love.[5]

But death interrupted and deflected her jauntiness.
When Catharine was sixteen, her mother died, and the
young girl, left to a "dark and dubious night," assumed
the responsibilities of womanhood. She made the clothes
for the younger children; prepared the doughnuts, grog,
and all the "fixings" for the minister's wood-spell; and
composed the stiff letter with which the children greeted
their elegant new stepmother a year later. So the young

[5] *The Autobiography of Lyman Beecher*, edited by Barbara M.
Cross (Cambridge, Mass., 1961), I, 104, 106.

Catharine adjusted to her loss through labor and responsibility; she kept her intimacy with her father, and she regained her high spirits. When she was eighteen, the "soft and perfumed air" around Boston made her so "*mad* with delight" that she "climbed on the rocks and *shouted* for joy"; at the age of twenty-one, she was exchanging "queer" letters, full of "spunk," with a young Yale professor, Alexander Metcalf Fisher. In 1822, an engagement was arranged, to Lyman Beecher's glee, and Catharine saw herself headed for an honored domesticity as the wife of "the greatest mathematician and philosopher in the country!"[6]

As she stood on the verge of a new life, however, Catharine was again balked by death. In 1823, her fiancé was killed in a shipwreck. Neither Catharine nor her father could find evidence that Fisher had known saving grace; and Catharine faced a grim, more final loneliness, as she arraigned her father's God and prepared herself for spinsterhood. The Calvinist economy made the death appear as a providential judgment upon her happiness and as a tocsin for change. "I am not what I was," she wrote accurately; "I never shall be again." She turned her liveliness to habits of command; people no longer associated her with "a constant stream of mirthfulness." Yet, even as an old lady, she kept the childish corkscrew curls that incongruously framed her heavy features and her sallow skin. A vociferous and bossy guest, bent upon a public service of impersonal benevolence, she lived chiefly in other people's houses. She worked incessantly, haranguing, planning, repeating herself, spending her income on

[6] *Ibid.*, p. 227; Catharine E. Beecher to Louisa Waite, March, 1821, and Catharine E. Beecher to Lyman Beecher, June, 1821 (Women's Archives at Radcliffe College [referred to as Radcliffe College Archives henceforward]).

her philanthropic projects, fighting for other women luckier than herself. Only periodic breakdowns, when the performance of any duty brought "extreme pain and such confusion of thought as seemed like insanity," interrupted her resolute service. She elected the costly virtue of renunciation, doing always "what, as to personal taste, I least wished to do." Like her father, who published his letters to his bereaved daughter as a model of New England divinity, Catharine plucked her experience for the instruction of others. As she shoved privacy and joy behind her, she set herself, her loss, and her convictions upon the public stage; in deliberate repudiation of the personal, she made her memories serve her cause and turned her nostalgia into a program for the nation.[7]

So Catharine Beecher set about finding the widest "sphere of influence" available to a single woman. In 1824, she opened a girls' school in Hartford, which austerely limited its curriculum to "the most necessary parts of education" and charged extra fees for music and dancing. Though the school grew rapidly, by 1832 Catharine was glad to join her family in a move to Cincinnati, where her father hoped to build a bulwark of evangelical Protestantism and where she headed the Western Female Institute. But she soon went after bigger game. To her father and to herself, Fisher's death finally seemed a sign that she had been reserved for some special mission, and she devised a strenuous gospel from the past she could never recover. Though the process of moral publicity emptied the past of its insouciance and warmth, she fastened the more fiercely upon her useful memories.

[7] Catharine E. Beecher to Louisa Waite, January, 1823 (Radcliffe College Archives); Harriet Beecher Stowe, quoted in *The Autobiography of Lyman Beecher*, I, 396; Catharine E. Beecher, *Educational Reminiscences and Suggestions* (New York, 1874), p. 58.

Echoing her father's note of apocalyptic urgency, she called upon American women to save their nation and the world by honoring their peculiar womanly duties as nurses, teachers, and mothers. Her program sprang from indignation at a society so awry that "to be the nurse of young children, a cook, or a housemaid is regarded as the last and lowest resort of poverty"; and she tartly recalled her readers to the era when women were judged by their "faculty" and intuitively knew the cheapest, healthiest, and tastiest foods.[8]

Miss Beecher had circulated a questionnaire among middle-class wives, and the responses convinced her that most of them suffered from invalidism, spasms, backache, or neurasthenia. She found that the agonies of childbirth, nursing, and motherhood made women despair at the birth and marriage of daughters; and she worked to replace the languishing, corseted lady of wealth, the worn, extravagant housewife, and the "fainting, weeping, vapid, pretty plaything" of society with an energetic and enlightened figure, clad "in the panoply of Heaven and sending the thrill of benevolence through a thousand youthful hearts." Her concern was always the restitution of a home where work, health, and frugality ensured immediate and eternal happiness and where family comforts were never sacrificed to elegance, nor space for kitchens and nurseries to "expensive piazzas." She demanded that the dark, isolated kitchen be replaced by a large sunny room, where both cooking and family life could be enjoyed and where women might be dressed gracefully for both housework and society. In her household blueprints, the entire first floor was given over to the

8 Catharine E. Beecher to Lyman Beecher, February, 1823 (Radcliffe College Archives); Catharine E. Beecher and Harriet Beecher Stowe, *The American Woman's Home* (New York, 1869), p. 13.

"Family Room" and the "Home Room," while parlor and library were squeezed together on the second floor. Since her idyl of domestic life could not accommodate "coarse and vulgar" immigrant servants, who lived in the cellar and slept in the attic, who ruined food in the kitchen and children in the nursery, she tried to get such strangers out of the home and to replace them with diligent children and coping wives.[9]

Imbuing home and mother with a holiness that would have appalled her Presbyterian father and her Puritan ancestors, Catharine Beecher helped her century invest the more matter-of-fact domesticity of the past with a sacred terror. For though Cotton Mather, Jonathan Edwards, and Lyman Beecher had taken their duties as heads of households seriously, they had characteristically thought in terms of family government, not family beatitude. Only in the nineteenth century—in the rhetoric of gift books and best sellers like *The Mother at Home,* in popular manuals on home building like Andrew Jackson Downing's *Architecture of Country Houses,* in the arguments of ministers like Horace Bushnell and educators like Catharine Beecher—did the family emerge as the *imago dei.* To Catharine Beecher, the family seemed the incarnation and the seedbed of Christian virtue. For the family was founded on the law of sacrifice, and within its economy the wife and mother engaged in the continual humiliation, service, and selfless love that had constituted Christ's work and command. Accepting the lowliest, least prestigious tasks—serving the weak, the ill,

---

[9] Catharine E. Beecher, *Suggestions Respecting Improvements in Education* (Hartford, Conn., 1829), pp. 53–54, 129; Beecher and Stowe, *The American Woman's Home,* p. 165 and *passim;* Catharine E. Beecher, "How to Redeem Woman's Profession from Dishonor," *Harper's New Monthly Magazine,* XXXI (1865), 710–716.

and the young—woman made her life an imitation of Christ: "Her grand mission is self-denial." For the many Americans instructed in New England Calvinism, the injunction possessed an august exigency; from the time of Jonathan Edwards, Presbyterian and Congregational theologians had discovered in such selfless benevolence the distinguishing mark of the elect.[10] Though educators like Mary Lyon and Emma Willard shared her conviction that woman's profession was one of service, only Catharine Beecher incorporated this imperial vision of woman's role into books of recipes, household hints, and physiology.

Miss Beecher based her grand claims for the wife and mother upon the psychology of the Scottish common-sense realists, which dominated nineteenth-century American texts in moral and mental philosophy and which taught that childhood associations between particular sensations and the experience of pleasure or pain largely determine character. Like Horace Bushnell, Horace Mann, and the authors of many best sellers on child care, Miss Beecher announced the power of nurture, which could make "the ill-natured amiable, the selfish regardful of the feelings and rights of others, the obstinate yielding and docile." She joined this doctrine of childhood plasticity to other theories which stressed the supreme powers of the mother but which assumed that these powers were based upon physiology. All future "feelings, thoughts, and volitions" were determined by the food particles that passed through children's brains. Able to regulate the air, the clothing, the

10 Beecher, *Educational Reminiscences and Suggestions*, p. 48. Edwardsian divines like Samuel Hopkins and Lyman Beecher identified virtue with a benevolence in which there was no trace of self-interest; Edwards himself had discussed the concept in his essay on "The Nature of True Virtue."

food, and the hours of the family, the mother was "sovereign of an empire." Whether their children went west to farm or cityward to prosper, the many readers of Miss Beecher's books could comfort themselves with the thought that no child would ever lose the imprint of his mother's enlightened goodness. Thus, the sanctification of the bourgeois home served a nation of wanderers. In the 1830's, de Tocqueville noted that Americans had "no adolescence," since "at the close of boyhood the man appears and begins to trace out his own fate." The confident love of mothers who always knew the "right thing" to do could give a sense of stability to children soon on the move; and in the loneliness of their freedom, these boy-men might find security and constraint in the memory of their mothers' tireless sacrifices.[11]

Miss Beecher spoke, too, to the dread and grief of bereaved parents in a time of high infant mortality. The literature of the gift annuals might assuage the grief through the rhetoric and iconography of sentiment, but Miss Beecher set about to eradicate the dread through know-how. *Hearth and Home, Physiology and Calisthenics,* and *The American Woman's Home* bristled with moralized information that could turn the diffident housewife into a formidable authority. The popularity of the books suggests that there had been some lapse in the training of the young and that faced with arranging *petits soupers* for hundreds, with Irish servants, and with the strangeness of the city or frontier, young wives were both

[11] Beecher, *Educational Reminiscences and Suggestions,* p. 49; Beecher and Stowe, *The American Woman's Home,* p. 140; Catharine E. Beecher, *A Treatise on Domestic Economy, for the Use of Young Ladies at Home and at School* (New York, 1856), p. 157; Alexis de Tocqueville, *Democracy in America,* edited by Phillips Bradley (New York, 1945), II, 192; Erik H. Erikson, *Childhood and Society* (New York, 1950), pp. 250–251.

disturbed and baffled. Printed substitutes for domestic apprenticeship, the books tutored women in a new self-consciousness. Graphically exposing the structure of the body—"the twenty-eight miles of perspiration tubes," the "delicate and sensitive parts" made ulcerous by corsets, the "poisonous effluvia" of the skin—they described a world so scary that the guardian woman, standing between her brood and insanity, sickness, or death, was indeed awful and resplendent. Small bedrooms and air-tight stoves were "poisoning more than one-half of the nation"; excessive study, which drew the blood from the organs, was creating mentally disturbed children; babies were being killed by medicine and ignorant nurses. Patently the housekeeper mattered: it was up to her to provide the "hogshead of pure air every hour" that would save her family from "sleeplessness, nausea, apoplexy, and even death"; to ensure that teething infants escaped convulsions; and at the same time—though thus constantly threatened by ruin and mortality—to preserve her "good temper." For the Christian household had to be not only efficient but regenerative as well.[12]

Catharine Beecher spent the income from her books on educational projects that would implement her convictions. Certain that the former schoolteacher made the best wife, she worked to establish colleges where women could be trained for their intricate duties as nurses, housekeepers, and teachers. Through the Board of National Popular Education, founded in 1846, and the American Woman's Educational Association, founded

[12] Catharine E. Beecher, *Physiology and Calisthenics, for Schools and Families* (New York, 1859), pp. 86–87, 38; Beecher and Stowe, *The American Woman's Home*, p. 7 and *passim;* [Catharine E. Beecher], *The Duty of American Women to Their Country* (New York, 1845), pp. 40 ff.; Beecher and Stowe, *The American Woman's Home*, Chap. 16.

in 1852, she collected Eastern funds with which to send to the West teachers armed with her own *Domestic Economy*. She founded a permanent college in Milwaukee and two short-lived institutions in Iowa and Illinois. With shrewd ardor she fought for higher pay for teachers, institutional acknowledgment of the "discipline" of domestic economy, and recognition that society had to honor woman's "profession" if women were to do their work without humiliation and bitterness.

Catharine Beecher's books on domestic duties went through many editions. Other writers of best sellers shared her faith in the saving power of a mother's love; the popular gift books continually rhapsodized over motherhood. But Miss Beecher provided sentiment with a schedule, a program, and a confident self-righteousness. Erudite and handy, her American woman would know "how dampers and air-boxes should be placed and regulated, how to prevent or remedy gas escapes," and how to manage "ball corks and high and low pressure on water pipes." With such knowledge and through unflagging service, women would redeem the family and finally institute a "Pink and White Tyranny more stringent than any earthly thralldom."[13] Without effusing over "the heart," Catharine Beecher defined a woman's love as the care of others and assigned her to a vigilant and informed protectiveness. Refusing to discount any necessary work as mere drudgery, she concerned herself with the lives the majority of women were called upon to lead and attempted to convert the fearful wife or mother into a learned and faithful steward of many talents.

But though Miss Beecher's books were read, female institutes continued to offer numerous courses in "ele-

[13] Catharine E. Beecher and Harriet Beecher Stowe, *The New Housekeeper's Manual* (New York, 1873), pp. 14 ff.

gant accomplishments," and schools for domestic science and teacher training were not widely established until the twentieth century. Harriet Beecher Stowe's Little Eva, not George Eliot's Mrs. Poyser, held the American imagination. Forced to witness the irrelevant, nerve-wracking curricula of Smith and Vassar and the pointless agitation of suffragettes, Catharine Beecher kept on fighting; and at the age of seventy-eight, in the year of her death, she lectured to Elmira College students on "The Adaptation of Woman's Education to Home Life."

III

Even in her own time, Catharine Beecher's ideal seemed restrictive and ignominious to younger women raised in different traditions. Though Margaret Fuller, ten years Miss Beecher's junior, briefly deplored stale air and corsets, such matters bored her. Like the young men with whom she conversed and corresponded, Margaret Fuller was born "with a knife" in her brain, a "tendency to introversion, self-dissection, the anatomizing of motives." Her critique struck always inward; she lived in the glare of analysis, setting before herself and her small self-conscious circle the instructive mystery of feminine genius. "We have had no woman," Bronson Alcott testified, "approaching so near our conception of the ideal woman as herself."[14] The role was taxing and was itself a kind of career. So for her contemporaries and for the future, Margaret Fuller's writings counted less than her personality, which she ruthlessly probed, arraigned, and publicized.

14 *The Complete Works of Ralph Waldo Emerson,* edited by Edward Waldo Emerson (Boston, 1903–1904), X, 327, 329; *The Journals of Bronson Alcott,* edited by Odell Shepard (Boston, 1938), p. 410.

For Margaret Fuller, the first step in education was the achievement of self-knowledge. She maintained that the classical education which her father had forced upon her as a child had only muffled her true self "under the thick curtain of available intellect," and throughout her life she resented the nightly recitations to him, which had left her sleepless and hallucinatory. If as an adult she labored at books as hard as he could have wished, she did not settle for erudition alone but avidly pursued the secret of herself—her motives, her grandeur, her privation. Upon consideration, she found no intellect in New England equal to her own; yet, at the age of thirty-six, she delighted in being called "a fool, little girl," by her elusive beloved, James Nathan. A troubled, ambiguous knowledge of herself informed her sense of the feminine, and her severe perceptions made the genial generalizations of an earlier generation seem glib.[15]

Margaret Fuller found the ideal of sacrifice that had inspired Catharine Beecher too constraining to be moral. "I have been too much absorbed today by others," she complained at Brook Farm. "It has almost made me sick." She saw in renunciation not a "piercing virtue" but a dreary waste; a middle-aged woman who had spent her maturity caring for her decrepit mother depressed her as a "bloodless effigy of humanity." She demanded total fulfillment, though she—who had early decided her lot was to be "bright and ugly"—knew at first hand how hard it was to achieve such fulfillment. Her habit of "incessantly opening and shutting her eyelids," her nasal voice, her "arching and undulating neck" repelled acquaintances; yet she requisitioned deference and craved love. Somehow the "wild beasts and reptiles" of her "great nature"

[15] *Memoirs of Margaret Fuller Ossoli* (Boston, 1852), II, 76, and I, 229; *Love-Letters of Margaret Fuller Ossoli, 1845–1846* (New York, 1903), p. 130.

—the childishness and the arrogance—had to be tamed. Like Catharine Beecher, she assumed that intellectual activity was at odds with true femininity: the "Woman in me," she decided, "kneels and weeps in tender rapture; the Man in me rushes forth but only to be baffled." So she required integrity and knew division, until life seemed to her a process of mutilation. "A tone of sadness was in her voice like the wail of the ocean," Emerson recorded. "And from my earliest acquaintance, I had a feeling as if someone cried *Stand from under!*"[16]

Rejecting the Christian terminology by which Catharine Beecher, Mary Lyon, and Lydia Sigourney had defined the ideal woman, refusing to see with "common womanly eyes," Margaret Fuller elected the role of genius and sibyl; and with all her harsh, nervous flamboyance, she set out to be the American Corinne. Still, she found herself sick to faintness at the sight of the savage bosom of Michelangelo's sibyl and knew it was an evil fate to have "a man's ambition" and a woman's heart. Desperate for the tenderness she knew she repelled, she accepted her exclusion from the usual woman's lot with an extravagant and bitter pride. The depressions and three-week migraine headaches seemed the price of her genius, the exactions of her betrayed sexuality. "This ache is like a bodily wound. . . . When I rise into one of those rapturous moods of thought . . . my wound opens again."[17]

A small group of New England intellectuals offered

16 *Memoirs of Margaret Fuller Ossoli*, I, 162; *The Works of Oliver Wendell Holmes* (Boston, 1891–1892), VIII, 241–242; *Memoirs of Margaret Fuller Ossoli*, II, 136; Ralph Waldo Emerson, Manuscript journal on Margaret Fuller (Ralph Waldo Emerson Memorial Association collection [referred to as RWEMA henceforward]). Quotations from the RWEMA are published by courtesy of the Houghton Library, Harvard University.

17 *Memoirs of Margaret Fuller Ossoli*, I, 98, 229, 197.

her the categories and attitudes that enabled her partially to order her divided nature. Emerson first awakened her to the "inward life," and with him and the "stiff, heady, and rebellious band" that gathered around him, she found a way to be. She joined Alcott, Emerson, Thoreau, the Ripleys, Theodore Parker, and Frederic Hedge in an ardent revolt against everything that limited the human spirit. Though they did not consider themselves a party, to their enemies and to posterity they were transcendentalists; they shared the certainty that man's greatness outpaced his history and that once he was transfigured by a divine quickening, he would be free. Their vague and lofty presumptions, their exacting pieties, their watchful intimacies appealed to Margaret. "I wish, I long to be human," she announced to James Nathan, "but divinely human." In the dedication of these "fanatics in freedom," she found a vocation for herself and for all those worthy of being women. Though "blighted without," she had found "all being" at the center of herself; the inner world, with its majestic simplicity, was the only thing that counted. Writing to Channing from Europe, Margaret did not bore him with descriptions of famous people and "magnificent shows." "All these things are only to me an illuminated margin on the text of my inward life. I like only what little I find that is transcendently good."[18]

For the "bright and ugly" young girl, the high-minded obliviousness of the transcendentalists provided a certain security; yet their resolute spirituality could be ha-

[18] *Ibid.*, p. 194; *The Complete Works of Ralph Waldo Emerson*, X, 327; *Love-Letters of Margaret Fuller Ossoli*, p. 21; Margaret Fuller Ossoli, *Life Without and Life Within* (Boston, 1859), p. 331; Mason Wade, *Margaret Fuller: Whetstone of Genius* (New York, 1940), p. 203.

rassing. The transcendentalist genius could not brook drudgery, and Margaret saw the "low neutralizing cares" of maternity, babies, and housekeeping as impertinences to the spirit. At first, she dismayed Emerson by making him laugh at her satiric gossip; but she learned the high transcendentalist note, and her comic bent was duly curbed to New England's willed and censorious innocence. "I look to Concord as my Lethe and Ennoe after this Purgatory of distracting petty tasks," she wrote to Emerson after the failure of Alcott's experimental school, where she had been teaching; "I am sure you will purify and strengthen me to enter the Paradise of thought once more." Accountable for high seriousness, for solitary joys, and for a penetrating originality, the transcendentalists checked up on themselves and on each other. In 1843, Emerson was gratified to discover that Margaret had risen to a visibly "higher state" since their last meeting; she, on the other hand, accused him of being always "on stilts." There were many pitfalls: Margaret felt guilty for her chronic apathy toward spiritual subjects; yet she had to guard against the "intoxication" of Emerson's presence, which made her giddy and dependent.[19]

Margaret Fuller began her career as disciple of the transcendentalists' strenuous idealism, and in 1844, she set forth her program for women in *Man and Woman: The Great Lawsuit*. She had found that her own law was "incapable of a charter," and she urged her sex to a similar emancipation. Her fundamental argument was that every conventional limitation upon woman betrayed her,

[19] *Memoirs of Margaret Fuller Ossoli*, I, 293; *The Complete Works of Nathaniel Hawthorne*, edited by George Parsons Lathrop (Boston, 1883), IX, 334; *Journals of Ralph Waldo Emerson*, edited by Edward Waldo Emerson and Waldo Emerson Forbes (Boston, 1909–1913), V, 324.

since spirit knew no sex. Woman could learn her sacred
independence and develop her latent powers only in
liberty. The "weakening habit" of dependence had to be
broken, for it had led to an "excessive devotion," which
destroyed love and degraded marriage. If a wife was
subordinate to her husband, her slavery would twist the
lives of both. At present, there was "no Woman, only an
overgrown child." The privileges granted women were
insults, and their powers were corrupting. By controlling
daily comforts, by relentless chattering, by exploiting the
weapons of the servile—"cunning, blandishment, and
unreasonable emotion"—women could subjugate their
husbands. But Margaret Fuller's long exposure to her
own buried motives made her mistrust the gentility of a
"Pink and White Tyranny."[20]

Though the popular literature of the time celebrated
the sanctity of the family, Margaret Fuller described the
bourgeois household as bleak and dreary. She saw desperate "good wives" trying to escape their boredom and their
families by attending "balls, theaters, meetings for pro-
moting missions, and revival meetings." Convinced that
the primary crime was interfering with the flow of creative energy, she announced that the central evil of her
society was its sexual code. Many were forced to celibacy;
yet she found spinsters and bachelors repulsive, "inhuman and inhumane." Taught that passion was revolting
and that their husbands' lust had to be quickly gratified,
young women inevitably became disturbed and squea-
mish wives. The women of genius—a Mary Wollstonecraft
or a George Sand—were turned into outlaws by society's restrictive sexual code, but Margaret Fuller saw

[20] *Memoirs of Margaret Fuller Ossoli*, II, 10; S. Margaret Fuller,
Woman in the Nineteenth Century (New York, 1845), pp. 119–122,
175–180, and *passim*.

George Sand's many love affairs as the necessary expression of her great nature. Her attack was radical and arrogant, the work of one who could announce that she did "not believe in society."[21] Secure in the queer high freedom of mid-nineteenth-century New England, she—unlike Catharine Beecher and M. Carey Thomas—dared relate woman's happiness to her sexual fulfillment.

While Catharine Beecher began her analysis with woman in society, Margaret Fuller started with an antecedent, prescriptive meeting between the individual spirit and the Muse. Woman's proper education began with a return to her original freedom. Only in separation could she recover her relationship to the sacred central energy from which her obligations sprang. Appropriating Emerson's vision of true manhood, Margaret made a feminist warcry of it; woman, like man, was the "channel through which heaven flows to earth," and she had only to claim her privileges. The encounter with the Muse, like antinomian faith, freed the initiate from bondage to convention. By hastily assuming the role of wife, housekeeper, teacher, or nurse, woman betrayed the freewheeling divinity that was the source of true life. The primary duty of women was to attune themselves to the discoveries of solitude; then "let them be sea-captains."[22]

All Margaret Fuller's pedagogical theories sprang from her faith in the freed intelligence. Though she read "at a rate like Gibbon's," though she mailed Emerson more volumes than he bothered to unwrap, she saw her studies only as a means to becoming an *"Original Genie."* For children, she recommended an education that followed,

[21] *Ibid.*, pp. 35 ff.; *Memoirs of Margaret Fuller Ossoli*, II, 58.
[22] *The Complete Works of Ralph Waldo Emerson*, II, 198–217; Fuller, *Woman in the Nineteenth Century*, pp. 178 ff.; quoted in Arthur W. Brown, *Margaret Fuller* (New York, 1964), p. 76.

rather than preceded, their experience. Rather than being moralized or "monotonously tender," children's books should present the facts of history and nature with provocative directness, thus instilling in their readers a sense of "vast mysteries." Memorization and too much reading hindered the emergence of the passionate individuality that was each child's birthright.[23]

Harassed throughout her life by the necessity of earning money, Margaret Fuller for a time, and with some reluctance, tried out her theories in the classroom. She taught languages at Alcott's Temple School and in 1837 became a principal teacher at the experimental Greene Street School in Providence, where she omitted many things customarily thought indispensable in education but slowly taught her sixty pupils to walk in "new paths." She insisted that her students "*talk* as well as *recite*," puzzled them with a definition of poetry full of terms like "imagination" and "ideality," cut them "up into bits," scared, perplexed, and inspired them. Yet despite her students' worship, she hated the schoolroom, which made her feel "vulgarized, profaned, forsaken"; and despite her need for money, she quit after a year and a half. "I do not wish to teach again," she wrote to Channing.[24]

Teaching had distracted Margaret from her primary duty of self-education, and her next occupation joined more closely her inner and her public callings. For the transcendentalists, the central ordeal was not parenthood, childhood, marriage, or education, but friendship, which made even the language of love seem "suspicious

---

[23] Fuller, *Woman in the Nineteenth Century*, pp. 310–313.

[24] *Memoirs of Margaret Fuller Ossoli*, I, 174–178; Harriet Johnson, "Margaret Fuller as Known by Her Scholars," *The Christian Register*, LXXXIX (1910), 426–428; Thomas Wentworth Higginson, *Margaret Fuller Ossoli* (Boston, 1884), p. 85.

and common." The subject was obsessive for them all, and throughout the 1840's, Emerson and Margaret made the concept an occasion for inquisition. Both knew how precious and exacerbating the relationship was. "The other night I found myself wishing to die because I had friends," Emerson wrote. Yet only the meetings between friends could bring a fleeting illumination and a brief release from solitude; marriage reduced the Elysian tables of friendship to fragmentary confidences "not worth picking up." The delicate equipoise of friendship proved the soul. Perhaps Margaret was too importunate; perhaps Emerson was disabled by his "porcupine impossibility of contact with men." Margaret accused him of turning their friendship into "trade." But neither would accept defeat. "I am no usurper," Margaret protested; "I ask only my own inheritance." In 1841, Emerson analyzed the austere offices of friendship in the *Dial*. "The solidest thing we know," friendship thrives where there is no "touching and clawing" but only the stark and sacred election of soul by soul. Friendship requires a prickly autonomy, and it does not bend to infirmities. "It treats its object as a god, that it may deify both." It was as the friend of chosen men and women that Margaret Fuller played her part and made her living in the Boston-Concord world. Presumptuous, rude, needy, she found a critical discipline in the role.[25]

By common testimony, Margaret Fuller had an oddly magnetic power; younger women revered her and told her "the most jealously guarded secrets of their lives" with an alacrity that irritated husbands like Hawthorne and Greeley. Sophia Peabody Hawthorne addressed her,

25 *The Letters of Ralph Waldo Emerson,* edited by Ralph L. Rusk (New York, 1939), II, 340; Ralph Waldo Emerson, *Essays: First Series* (Boston, 1865), II, 191–217.

in a series of sonnets, as "A Priestess of the Temple Not Made with Human Hands." Elizabeth Peabody kept a journal on her; Anna Ward "idolized" her. What Margaret Fuller offered the women who clustered about her was a stern lucidity. She did not traffic in the conventions that made Sophia Hawthorne a "dove" to her Nathaniel; she instructed the most benevolent of her friends with scathing candor. Thus, she informed the philanthropic and goodhearted Elizabeth Peabody that her "suffocating" friendships made her repulsive. With her piercing glance and "rudely searching words," she complimented women by bothering to "find them out." She made them feel that she knew their sad limitations, and they repaid her discrimination with devotion. Elizabeth Hoar told Emerson, who was bemused by Margaret's eventual romance, that any one of the "fine girls of sixteen" she knew would gladly have married her "if she had been a man," for she "understood them." With both men and women she insisted on a harrowing intimacy, which brought ecstatic "fusions" and abrupt recoilings. Emerson thought her too passionate, so she tried to repress her extravagant love, only to find herself even more "prodigal." Still, she and Emerson eventually agreed that she had risen above the "search after Eros," and by 1843, her friendship with him made his relationships with others seem like "trade." Whatever needs made her overweening, her conscious effort was always toward the achievement of true friendship, which would confer upon each friend a "clue to the labyrinth" of his being. As a friend, she detected the "Immortal under every disguise in every place" and inspired everyone with a fine discontent. As a friend, above all, she talked.[26]

[26] Horace Greeley, *Recollections of a Busy Life* (New York, 1868), p. 178; Emerson, Manuscript journal on Margaret Fuller; *The Let-*

The medium of friendship was conversation, and the little circle of friends set about conversing with resolute pride. Like the journal and letter, conversation could capture the quick play of the spontaneous spirit. It was for her talk that Margaret Fuller was noted, admired, and feared. Alcott thought her the best "talker" of the age; Orestes Brownson praised her conversation, in *The Quarterly Review*, as "brilliant, instructive, and inspiring"; to Emerson, her talk seemed the most entertaining in America. When Rufus Griswold wrote up "Sarah Margaret Fuller" in *The Prose Writers of America,* he praised her for her mastery of this form, which mid-nineteenth-century Americans prized.[27]

Margaret's talents and society thus enabled her to devise a new form of pedagogy. In 1839, she decided to offer a series of "conversations," which would afford an interested circle of women the chance to inquire earnestly: "What were we born to do? And how shall we do it?" She had never taken to solitude; ravenous always for the human encounter, she had a bent for dialogue, and in nothing perhaps was she more American than in her incorrigible faith in high talk. Though Elizabeth Barrett Browning could not quite grasp the genre of a paid conversation, a businesslike high-mindedness made sense to Bostonians. If the conversations cost as much as lyceum lectures, they reached more deliberately after the soul.

---

ters of James Freeman Clarke to Margaret Fuller, edited by John Wesley Thomas (Hamburg, 1957), p. 85; *The Writings of Margaret Fuller,* selected and edited by Mason Wade (New York, 1941), p. 571; *Journals of Ralph Waldo Emerson,* VI, 364–365; *The Letters of Ralph Waldo Emerson,* VI, 366.

27 Margaret Munsterberg, "Margaret Fuller Centenary," *The Boston Public Library Quarterly,* II (1950), 253; Rufus Wilmot Griswold, *The Prose Writers of America* (Philadelphia, 1847), p. 538; *Journals of Ralph Waldo Emerson,* VI, 366.

Twenty-five of the wives and daughters of ministers, professors, merchants, high-school teachers, and physicians
of the Boston area paid their fees. Many of them—Lydia
Maria Child, Eliza Rotch Farrar, Eliza Buckminster Lee,
and Ellen Hooper, among others—were themselves authors. Through the conversations, these educated women
were to avoid the vain "display" of learning and begin to
build "the life of thought upon the life of action." Planning to make "heroes" of them all, Margaret required
that these friends risk the ridicule of society, give up
haziness and "coterie criticism," and forage after truth
itself. Above all, they had to talk, for she would feel par-
alyzed by "general silence or side-talks."[28]

For five winters, from 1839 to 1844, Margaret Fuller
held her "conversation parties," in which about a third
of the group took an active part. Desiring a topic "playful as well as deep," "serious" but not "solemn," she
chose Greek mythology for the first subject, since she was
after the game of intellect, not a provincial partisan-
ship. The tone was set by Margaret, who was coquet-
tish, scolding, arch, or oracular. She opened each conversation with an outline of the subject under discussion;
after her presentation, the group speculated and listened.
It was not always easy going. At first, she had trouble getting the ladies to discuss beauty—"They would not attend
to principles, but kept clinging to details"—and for a time

---

[28] *Memoirs of Margaret Fuller Ossoli,* I, 325–327; *The Letters of
Elizabeth Barrett Browning,* edited by Frederic G. Kenyon (London,
1897), I, 460. She characterized them redundantly as "oral lectures,"
to her an unfortunate form of publicity. The conversations cost
$16 for twenty-four hour and a quarter lessons with a class of
twenty-five; for a smaller group, meeting six times for two and a
half hours, the fee was $25. Margaret Fuller could not afford to
talk for nothing, since she had herself to support and her mother
to help out.

she let beauty "drop." Caroline Sturgis might prepare for a snooze, or Elizabeth Hoar might find the evening theatrical. But Margaret was pleased to have evoked "the tone of simple earnestness."[29]

Except when the presence of Emerson and other "untrained gentlemen" disturbed the "poetry" of the occasion, Margaret dominated the discussions, leaving her students impressed by her "beautiful modesty" and by their private discoveries. Sophia Peabody kept a record not of what was said but of her "impressions"; and in *Margaret and Her Friends*, a book reporting one season's meetings, Caroline Healey recounted her own unspoken thoughts as meticulously as she recorded the comments of Margaret, Emerson, and Alcott. In all the available accounts of the meetings, two people are central, Margaret and the writer. Margaret's techniques encouraged the ladies to heroic generalizations, and their dogged and blithe inquisitiveness gave the meetings a kind of spectral liveliness.[30]

In their gaudy moralizing, the ladies combined the exotic and the homely; and Bacchus, Ceres, Apollo, and Prometheus took on the more familiar shapes of Geniality, Productive Energy, Genius, and Pure Reason. No reading was required, for moral intuition provided a short cut to knowledge. Margaret announced that the puzzling marriage of Venus and Mercury must be an interpolation, since there could be "*no* affinities between love and craft." She moved quickly to the largest view and recapitulated the gist of a talk with vigorous finality. Thus, she summed up an evening conversation: "The

[29] Margaret Fuller to Ralph Waldo Emerson, November, 1839, and Elizabeth Hoar to Ralph Waldo Emerson, March, 1841 (RWEMA); *Memoirs of Margaret Fuller Ossoli*, I, 3, 325.

[30] *The Letters of Ralph Waldo Emerson*, II, 361, 384; *Memoirs of Margaret Fuller Ossoli*, I, 312.

Indomitable Will had dethroned Time, and acting with Productive Energy . . . had driven back the sensual passions to the bowels of the earth." A few members risked skittish parallels with Christianity. Subjects that touched on the controversial or contemporary—creeds, women, Catholicism—proved unsuccessful. Yet the little band managed to tackle topics at once puzzling and obliquely germane. To one participant, the conversations suggested Platonic dialogue; for another, Margaret Fuller exposed "the book of life." "Whatever she spoke of revealed a hidden meaning. . . . I was no longer the limitation of myself," Ednah Dow Cheney recalled, "but I felt the whole wealth of the universe was open to me."[31]

Though the excitement of the conversations often left her sleepless, Margaret found the work "sweet." Swept by a power "higher than her own," she saw herself as a prophetess, who turned the humdrum material of her students to her own ends and flashed such transfiguring "rays of truth" upon the familiar that her "startled" audience went "on their way rejoicing in the slight glimpse" of wisdom they had caught. If her hopes for her pupils were thus modest, she felt that she herself had at last enjoyed a "real society." By and large, her friends approved of her experiment in learning. To Emerson, the "conversation room" seemed, in the dreariness of the time, "the search of the best after the sun."[32]

[31] *Margaret and Her Friends, or, Ten Conversations with Margaret Fuller,* reported by Caroline W. Healey (Boston, 1895), p. 102; "Margaret Fuller to Sarah Helen Whitman," edited by Granville Hicks, *American Literature,* I (1930), 420; *The Letters of Ralph Waldo Emerson,* II, 353, and III, 221; Julia Ward Howe, *Margaret Fuller* (Boston, 1883), p. 109; *Reminiscences of Ednah Dow Cheney* (Boston, 1902), pp. 203–205.

[32] L. H. Boutell, "Margaret Fuller Ossoli," *The Chautauquan,* XI (1890), 700; "Margaret Fuller to Sarah Helen Whitman," p. 420; *The Letters of Ralph Waldo Emerson,* III, 214.

Pleased with her efforts, Margaret Fuller did not stop holding conversations, even after the Boston meetings had ended; and she saw her other work during the 1840's —as co-editor with Emerson of the *Dial* and as contributor to Greeley's New York *Tribune*—as similar to conversations. For, like talk, journals and newspapers spoke to the moment; they were impressionistic, volatile, accessible. The introduction to the *Dial*, written by Margaret and revised by Emerson, promised that the magazine would provide not the multiplication of books but a report on life: "Our resources are therefore not so much the pens of practised writers as the conversation [later changed to "discourse"] of the living and the portfolios which friendship has opened to us." Thus, Margaret Fuller continued her effort to open an urgent human colloquy and to grace it with the magnanimity of the impersonal. Emerson spurred her on, praising her article on the drama as elevated above ordinary writing and rejoicing that "the hardened sinners will be saved for your sake, O living friend!"[33]

In the last stage of her education, Margaret Fuller found herself again at the beginning. In 1846, she traveled to England and the continent. Like Henry James's American pilgrims, she first discovered through Europe how imprisoning a self-conscious rectitude might be. Unlike her contemporary, Nathaniel Hawthorne, who maintained a wary propriety in the labyrinth of Europe, Margaret Fuller proved herself capable of radical experience. Though Florence, which reminded her of Boston, struck her as "still and glum as death," Rome strangely illuminated "the whole bright house of her exposure." What she discovered was simply, as she informed Emerson, that she had wasted her life among "abstrac-

[33] *Ibid.*, II, 292; Emerson, Manuscript journal on Margaret Fuller.

tions." Thus, she dismissed her past—Emerson, friendship, conversations, and introspection—and with char-
acteristic violence set about educating herself in reality.
Though she no longer rehearsed the standard transcendentalist complaints about America's materialism, her
tone toward her native country was newly acerb. While
in Rome she decided that Americans were destitute not
of spirituality but of passion, and she duly warned the
conscientious American pilgrim that he could never understand the city. For it required something her com-
patriots lacked—the capacity for abandon. She took up
the cause of Mazzini, finding in the Italian struggle for
freedom an idealism absent in her own country. The
headiness she had indulged to "save her soul alive" in the
"unpropitious circumstances" of America was no longer
necessary; at last, she had discovered a propitious place
and time. As correspondent and as head of a hospital for
the wounded, she wrote in 1848: "If I came home at this
moment I should feel forced to leave my own house, my
own people, and the hour which I always longed for."[34]

All her earlier extravagance of passion and discipline
had come to seem "useless friction." Incredulous, Emerson heard of lovers: an Italian wanted to divorce so he
could marry Margaret, and Mazzini had proposed. In
1848, she had a child and was secretly married. Yet her
final emancipation did not bring happiness; the division
between her past and present life was too sharp, and she
could scarcely now obliterate some twenty years of New
England virtue. Her husband, Ossoli, was an impoverished Italian, with tenuous claims to nobility. He was ten

[34] *Memoirs of Margaret Fuller Ossoli*, II, 216; Margaret Fuller
Ossoli, *At Home and Abroad, or, Things and Thoughts in America
and Europe*, edited by Arthur B. Fuller (Boston, 1856), p. 232;
Henry James, *The Wings of the Dove* (New York, 1907), p. xxvi;
Memoirs of Margaret Fuller Ossoli, II, 225, 252.

years her junior, and she doubted that he would love her long. Incapable of speculating "about anything," ignorant, and without any "enthusiasm of character," he was in no way a "friend." When Margaret "conversed," he left the room. She knew that to her Boston circle her marriage would seem a curious betrayal, based, as Hawthorne sneered, on an attraction "purely sensual" and revealing that she was in the end only a woman, "strong and coarse." To Emerson, she knew, Ossoli would be "nothing." As for herself, she no longer planned on great achievements but made her "plea" with the Magdalen, that she had "loved much."[35]

In Rome, Margaret Fuller learned the extent of her earlier ignorance. Of maternity and experience she had known nothing, and her letters reiterate her abrupt and baffled humility. When her child was asleep beside her, she had the only hours of happiness she had ever known; she chronicled his smiles, his kicking, his feeding, his weight. But she could find no place for the woman she had become. Her husband's love, "in which there was all tenderness but no help," seemed inadequate. She planned to write a book on the birth of her child but had to stop, for it seemed to her that "he would die."[36]

In Italy, the republican cause had failed; there was nowhere to go but to America, where Margaret would have to support her husband and child. "With this year, I enter upon a sphere of my destiny so difficult that I, at present, see no way out except through the gate of

[35] Quoted in *Margaret Fuller: American Romantic,* edited by Perry Miller (Garden City, N.Y., 1963), p. 30; Emerson, Manuscript journal on Margaret Fuller; Julian Hawthorne, *Nathaniel Hawthorne and His Wife* (Boston, 1888), I, 259–262; *Memoirs of Margaret Fuller Ossoli,* II, 274, 276, 302.

[36] Quoted in *Margaret Fuller: American Romantic,* p. 283; *Memoirs of Margaret Fuller Ossoli,* II, 377.

death," she wrote to Caroline Sturgis. Her "tuition on this planet" now seemed complete. In 1848, with premonitions of death and praying only that she, her child, and her husband might live or die together, Margaret Fuller Ossoli embarked for America. The ship sank within sight of the New Jersey coast, and she apparently did not try to save either her own life or that of her family. Yet if Margaret—faced with a return to friendship—courted death in anticipation or act, her friends were loyal to the woman they thought they had known; when she died, Emerson felt he had lost his audience.[37]

In her program for women, as in her life, Margaret Fuller had relied solely upon the private sensibility, which recorded the lessons of analytical friendships, rash passions, and a harrowing self-consciousness. If she paid for her individualism by often seeming foolish, her life, with all its extravagance, finally achieved an exemplary seriousness. "What spoke unto the best among the years 1838 to 1842," Emerson mused on her death, "was the spontaneous and solitary thought." Yet, he added bitterly, her friends could conceive of no better use for the "most educated woman" America had produced than that married and impoverished, she should die "to save her board."[38]

IV

Martha Carey Thomas worked to provide talented women with institutions that would spare them the waste of solitude. Born in 1857, she disposed of problems with a briskness Margaret Fuller could never muster. Enlisting early in what she came to call "THE CAUSE," she

[37] *Journals of Ralph Waldo Emerson*, VIII, 117.
[38] *Ibid.*, p. 144; Emerson, Manuscript journal on Margaret Fuller.

did not squander her anger in self-hatred but charged against the society that consigned girls to inferior positions and occupations. Too definite and too practical to enjoy the equivocal illumination of self-doubt, she set out to expand the theater of women's lives. She put her faith in institutions, not in singular ecstasies or the home, and she consistently aligned herself with power. She made it her job to foster institutions which would equip women for service in the world and which would endow them with the knowledge, skills, and prestige previously reserved for men. What she wanted for women was nothing less than victory.

Her exuberant rage began early in her childhood. Pretty, boisterous, indulged, the oldest child in a prominent family of Maryland Quakers, Martha had always been bent on pre-eminence, and she resented the privileges granted her four younger brothers, her father, and the masculine sex in general. She poised her infuriated confidence against the conventional ranking of the sexes. "I believe I have as much sense as any boy I know . . . and more too," she asserted in her diary. As a young girl, she looked forward to a career righting the injustices that incensed her. "For a woman," she wrote, "there always remains stirring up women to revolt, waking up girls; it is delicious to plant theories of independence."[39]

Above all, Martha despised the roles and privileges of upper-class girls and women. Their parties and visiting, their philanthropies and large families appalled her: "More and more every day I'm making up my mind to be a doctor for when I grow up I can't be dependent on father and mother and I ain't going to get married and I don't want to teach school. . . . I can't imagine anything

[39] Edith Finch, *Carey Thomas of Bryn Mawr* (New York, 1947), pp. 32, 118.

worse than living a regular young lady's life. . . . I don't
care if everybody would cut me. I despise society, and I
detest girls." Her beautiful mother had eight other children; she gently dominated her charming husband and
was, by family reckoning, the president of nine philanthropic organizations. But the pattern of her life did not
tempt her favorite child, who judged her mother with
unsparing pity.[40]

When M. Carey Thomas was thirty-one, her mother
died of a breast cancer, and Carey convinced her sister
Helen that the illness had sprung from childbearing.
"Suckling at her breast, one after another," Helen agreed,
"we had given my mother a mortal wound."[41] Between
the frivolities of the society girl and the servitude of the
matron, Carey saw only waste in the lives open to women
like herself. It was her father's life that shaped her ambitions: he was a doctor, which she first dreamed of being; a scholar, which she militantly became; and—as
trustee of Johns Hopkins, Haverford, and Bryn Mawr—
a leader in higher education. So she repudiated the conventions that structured the careers of upper-class women
and elected for herself a celibate rebellion.

Like Catharine Beecher and Margaret Fuller, M. Carey
Thomas assumed a conflict between womanliness and
intellect, and she never hesitated as to her own allegiance.
With Quaker austerity, she saw sex as an irritating
distraction from the duties of service and self-improve-
ment. When she studied her father's physiology text-
books, she found herself "more thankful than ever" to be
a girl, since women could continually improve themselves, while men had always to contend with their ani-

---

[40] *Ibid.*, p. 36.
[41] Helen Thomas Flexner, *A Quaker Childhood* (New Haven,
Conn., 1940), p. 332.

mal lust. Sexual instincts, marriage, and children, she thought, interfered with women's higher achievements. As a girl, she had assessed the costs of maternity. "If a woman has children," she wrote, "I do not see but what she will have to, at least for some time, give up her work; and of all things taking care of children does seem the most utterly unintellectual." Disabling and irrelevant, sexuality was also vaguely terrifying to her; and as she read Michelet's *La Femme*, she was revolted at the thought that she herself might be "so vile and pathological a thing." But her most conscious fear was that the woman Michelet described could "never go to college."[42]

Unlike Margaret Fuller, M. Carey Thomas did not hurl herself against the universe but doggedly set to work. She was simply after "the best" for women, and her strengths as well as her limitations lay in the economy of her imagination. Though she fought hard, she never inquired deeply; and throughout her life, her battle was eased by her hearty acceptance of the "goods" of intellectualism: a B.A., graduate study abroad, a Ph.D., professional success. Her lucidity was so great that it amounted to simple-mindedness, and the thrust of her many certainties carried her toward solutions. As a child, she had wept for fear that God's curse on Eve might mean that women could not have a college education; she saw the Civil War as "fortunate" because it increased the number of women teachers. By the time she was ten, she "dreamed of college day and night."[43]

She was warned that a college education would scare

[42] Finch, *Carey Thomas of Bryn Mawr*, p. 75; M. Carey Thomas, "Present Tendencies in Women's College and University Education," *Educational Review*, XXV (1908), 65.

[43] M. Carey Thomas, Notes for an address, June, 1907 (Bryn Mawr College Archives).

away bachelors. She fancied it might make her a "sort of woman devil," but having decided that college offered the only escape from the conventional female lot, she accepted the rules of the game. According to her cousin Logan Pearsall Smith, the Baltimore clan found her desire for a college education as shocking a choice as a life of prostitution, but M. Carey Thomas was only enlivened by the opposition.[44] She and her mother wept until her father surrendered, and Miss Thomas entered the junior class of Cornell in 1876, spurning Vassar as an advanced female seminary. She was disappointed, as she was repeatedly to be, by the frivolity of the women students and by the drabness of much of the intellectual life, but she did not loiter for reconsiderations. In 1877, she applied for admission to the newly established graduate school at Johns Hopkins.

Hopkins proved frustrating. It required much labor and offered few rewards for women. Though Professor Basil Gildersleeve permitted her to sit behind a curtain to hear his lectures, her privileges did not outweigh her inconveniences. Despite her resolution, M. Carey Thomas was too gregarious, too ambitious, and too impatient to thrive on inconspicuous victories. Protracted study soon bored her. The practical humanitarianism, sociability, and quiet security of her family had prepared her for action. She was willing to work, but she required the give-and-take of personal relationships and was always ready to be distracted from her studies by the problems that sprang from her passionate friendships. She had enlisted in higher education primarily for the sake of women, and she depended upon rewards that would

[44] M. Carey Thomas, Notes for an address at the Bryn Mawr School, 1910 (Bryn Mawr College Archives); Logan Pearsall Smith, *Unforgotten Years* (London, 1938), pp. 89–90.

announce the capacities of her sex. At Hopkins, which excluded women from seminars, she was oppressed by the squandering of her life. "I have no time to read, no time to see people. . . . It is a kind of living death."[45] Much as she feared hurting her cause, she withdrew from the university after a year, with ambitious plans for solitary study.

But her retreat to privacy was short-lived. She found her family stifling, and they found her difficult. In 1879, she set out with her beloved friend, the brilliant and nervous Mamie Gwynn, to study in Germany. Like many American students in the late nineteenth century, M. Carey Thomas discovered in the German university a model for the scholarly life. At the University of Leipzig, she enjoyed the rigors of foreign study, the dedication of the professors, and the enthusiasm of students "taking notes without a breath between." Thenceforth, she was one of the initiate. She found the romance and culture of Europe exhilarating; she "did" the museums and churches, dismissed the male students as dull, and labored at philology. But she did not neglect her primary purpose. Since neither Leipzig nor Göttingen gave the doctorate to women, Miss Thomas went to Zurich, where in 1882 she received her degree *summa cum laude* for a dissertation on *Sir Gawain and the Green Knight*. As she revised the manuscript for publication, she became appalled at having spent her time on such tedious and petty work, but she was proud of her honors and was ready to exploit them for her cause. So when she thought of the new college at Bryn Mawr, which had been provided for in the will of the Quaker Joseph Taylor, she was ready to propose herself for the presidency. Her father and uncle were serving as trustees of the new college, and,

[45] Finch, *Carey Thomas of Bryn Mawr*, p. 72.

with a confidence nurtured by an understanding of the politics of power, she wrote to her family: "I should love to have the presidency of Bryn Mawr. I believe I could make it the very best woman's college there is . . . and I do not believe any other person . . . would have the interests of other women so at heart, and, at the same time, would have the requisite training to enable her or him to see what was needed."[46]

In 1883, the trustees appointed a retired Quaker physician, Dr. James Rhoads, to the presidency and made M. Carey Thomas dean and professor of English; in 1894, when President Rhoads resigned, she was elected president by a majority of one. As dean and president, she at last had the opportunity to work for "THE CAUSE," and she harnessed her talents and her energy to the task. By the time her presidency had ended, the "college woman" had emerged upon the American scene as a distinct and privileged species of femininity. In the early twentieth century, the majority of women seeking a college education had been from the middle classes; by the end of M. Carey Thomas' career, going to college had become the "thing to do" for upper-class women as well. As much as any single person, M. Carey Thomas had been responsible for this change.

Miss Thomas publicized, commended, and to a great extent created the image of the "college woman," who was at last to justify her own belligerent pride. By the mid-1890's, the "Bryn Mawr student" had been written up in periodicals like *Godey's Lady's Book* and *The Home Maker;* in 1899, when Miss Thomas rebuked Harvard's President Charles W. Eliot for the "sun spots" on his brain, newspapers in Chicago, Salt Lake City, and Boston reported on the "Bryn Mawr woman." Through

[46] *Ibid.,* pp. 99, 129.

weekly chapel talks, addresses, and private interviews with each freshman, Miss Thomas engraved upon generations of undergraduates her ideal of the "Bryn Mawr student." She knew what she was after. In 1935, at the college's fiftieth anniversary celebration, she quoted the alumna letter she had prized most: "I have forgotten everything I learned at Bryn Mawr but I still see you standing in chapel and telling us to believe in women."[47]

Miss Thomas was determined from the first that Bryn Mawr should be the best women's college in the country. Rigorous entrance examinations were to enforce the high standards of the college, intimidate the lazy, and lure the ambitious. The college would include a graduate department, so that the undergraduates could glimpse the arcanum of scholarship and the faculty could engage in the original research she herself had found so deadly. Unlike Mount Holyoke students, Bryn Mawr girls would not drudge at housework; their only cares would be scholarly. Above all, Miss Thomas opposed special courses for women; their training was to be as rigorous and impractical as that provided at Harvard. She saw no way to educate women to be wives and mothers; for her, the world of intellect was above sex.

She found the assignment the more congenial since it meant war. By the end of the nineteenth century, Catharine Beecher's bogy of the intellectual female loomed newly fearsome. To medical writers and educationists writing in the *North American Review, Popular Science Monthly,* and the *Educational Review,* to intellectuals like Henry Adams and G. Stanley Hall, the learned woman threatened not only the American home but the very survival of the race. Turning an energy properly

[47] M. Carey Thomas, *Address at the Fiftieth Anniversary of Bryn Mawr College* (Bryn Mawr, Pa., n.d.), p. 54.

altruistic and collective into individualistic self-consciousness, deflecting blood to the brain from the "generative organs," with atrophied mammary glands and irregular periodicity, she had lost touch with the sacred primitive rhythms that bound her to "the deepest law of the cosmos." Immigrant women had many children and a low mortality rate, while college graduates, marrying late, if at all, produced small and nerve-ridden families."[48]

In place of the rigid, irrelevant curriculum of women's colleges, the psychologist G. Stanley Hall proposed a program organized around the monthly "Sabbath" of menstruation and centered on the dance, which he considered both a "mode of worship" and a "school of morals." For Hall, as for Adams, the acme of femininity was the "madonna conception," and, like Adams, he dreaded the race suicide that the sexless, neurotic modern woman portended. But at Bryn Mawr, the central ritual was Lantern Night, on which sophomores handed the "light of learning" to freshmen; and, as the prototype of the college that gave no quarter to sex, Bryn Mawr was closely scrutinized. In 1908, the *Educational Review* reported that of the students who had graduated from Bryn Mawr in 1890 only 25 per cent were married. Annoyed by Miss Thomas' claim that a woman's greatest happiness lay in "congenial work," *The Ladies' Home Journal* reminded readers in 1913 that what men liked most in women was milk.[49]

Such criticisms helped M. Carey Thomas clarify her own ideals; she was ready to back a new kind of woman, a new kind of marriage, a new concept of the relationship between education and life. Disturbed only by the

[48] G. Stanley Hall, *Adolescence* (New York, 1904), II, 595, 627.
[49] *Ibid.*, pp. 639–640; The Editor's Column, *The Ladies' Home Journal*, XXX (January, 1913), 21.

charge that a liberal arts education undermined a woman's health and fertility, she countered her opponents' statistics with national surveys which showed that the college woman's family outdid that of the average woman by a "fraction of a baby." And she gladly delineated what the New York *Tribune* called the "new Bryn Mawr woman." In 1908, she described the conventional woman as "chaste and loving and infinitely sympathetic and tender," sheltered from the "EVIL PASSIONS," and she dismissed her as ineffective and a little foolish. College overcame the innocence of sweet sixteen by giving students the chance to drink "of the enchanted cup of knowledge."[50]

President Eliot's complaint that a liberal arts education had nothing to do with a woman's future life did not irk Miss Thomas, for she treasured this very irrelevance. Cut off from past and future, the four years of college were the only time in a woman's life when she could devote herself exclusively to intellect. Never again would she be so free from the "dulling effects of financial or social responsibility" and from "sentimental and emotional disturbances." Like Henry James, M. Carey Thomas saw the American college as a monastery which, despite the surrounding "wilderness of the commercial," might initiate the young into the discipline of learning. For four years the student stood in the presence of unworldly dedication, witnessing the "halo" that encircled her teachers. The tranquillity of Bryn Mawr's Gothic architecture and Oxonian campus "civilized" the students, who came from all over the country, and freed them, as they walked under maple trees, for those "thoughts and dreams" that constituted the "college

[50] M. Carey Thomas, Notes for commencement addresses at Bryn Mawr College, 1904 and 1908 (Bryn Mawr College Archives).

idea." Such a remote world could not accommodate vo-
cational courses, which, suggesting the grind of domesticity or money-making, produced drab students and dreary
professors.[51]

The college existed to reveal a splendid mystery, and,
with her luxuriant rhetoric, President Thomas called
upon Bryn Mawr students to recognize their rare privileges. The four years of college, cutting them off from
their past and their future, were one of the few "really
great experiences of life." At college the "young Siegfried forges his sword; like the Nibelung cave it is a
little withdrawn from the outer World." The students
responded: they wore their caps and gowns to classes,
requested that the faculty teach in academic robes, and
impressed reporters with their erudite daily teas. They
were impressed themselves: in 1888, an English student
described Bryn Mawr in *The Nineteenth Century*, deli-
cately boasting of the students' luncheon discussions of
Grimm's Law and of their student government, with its
house of commons, prime minister, and sergeant at arms.
In 1898, the college literary magazine celebrated the new
creatures they were, disparaging the "Grecian girls in
robes of snow" and the "satin girls of long ago" beside

> The new maid ye cannot know
> In cap and gown.[52]

For these "four most impressionable years" of a woman's life Miss Thomas was ready to assume full responsi-

[51] M. Carey Thomas, Notes for the opening address at Bryn Mawr
College, 1899 (Bryn Mawr College Archives); Henry James, *The
American Scene* (New York, 1907), pp. 56, 69.

[52] M. Carey Thomas, Notes for the opening address at Bryn Mawr
College, 1903 (Bryn Mawr College Archives); Alys W. Pearsall
Smith, "A Women's College in the United States," *The Nineteenth
Century*, XXIII (1888), 920–921.

bility, and she warned students not to divide their hearts or their brains between home and college but to submit totally to the Bryn Mawr influence. One task of Bryn Mawr was the loosening of the family unit Catharine Beecher had celebrated. As an institution, the college had to emancipate the young girl from her typical social roles. To get away from their society mothers, students were to reside at the college and have limited weekends and short vacations. Miss Thomas was well satisfied when Bryn Mawr girls refused to tolerate "old fashioned untrained matrons" as housemothers and required instead that these maternal figures have B.A. degrees, preferably from Bryn Mawr.[53]

The college was "the nursing mother of women yet unborn"; its brood was to speak elegantly, without "uncouth pronunciations," and be well mannered, punctual, and clean. President Thomas lectured to the students on daily baths and on breeding for a superior race, and she encouraged those from less fortunate homes to learn the "Bryn Mawr way" from their more privileged sisters. Not every girl was capable of becoming a "Bryn Mawr woman," and so she advised the lazy, the plodding, and those who wanted an "American good time" to make room for the "true Bryn Mawr type." The type was special: President Thomas congratulated her students on being Anglo-Saxon Protestants, the "delicate flowers" produced by centuries of breeding.[54]

The "new woman" would transform the traditional patterns of romance, marriage, and the family by creat-

[53] M. Carey Thomas, Notes for the opening address at Bryn Mawr College, 1921 (Bryn Mawr College Archives); Thomas, "Present Tendencies in Women's College and University Education," p. 68.

[54] M. Carey Thomas, Notes for the opening address at Bryn Mawr College, 1901 (Bryn Mawr College Archives); M. Carey Thomas, in *The Bryn Mawr Alumnae Quarterly* (November, 1917), p. 2.

ing a new equality and a new kind of union. The college-educated couple would be working comrades. President Thomas counseled undergraduates to marry men whose fastidious habits, decorum, and intellectual training they shared. The college-educated husband would not be baffled by any "mystery" in his college-educated wife. Since they would argue from the same premises, they would reach the same conclusions; and they would always be able to subordinate their sexuality to an intellectual union. Whereas French marriages foundered on suspicion, the college-educated husband and wife, guided by similar morals and similar scholarly ideals, would meet as equals, serene in their common knowledge and mutual respect. President Thomas predicted that eventually the college alumna would rebel against the dreariness of housework and pay for domestic services with money earned in more interesting work. Given the small size of their families, college women would not have any excuse to linger at home as "mothers," once their children were in school, but would seize the chance to leave their housework and use their minds again. One way or another, the potential earning power of the college-educated woman would be utilized. As a result, she would become so tempting a catch that not 50 but 100 per cent of the nation's female B.A.'s would marry; men of moderate incomes would not be able to afford to marry any other women.[55]

But the model Bryn Mawr graduate did not choose the common female lot. The "superwomen" who became scholars, doctors, architects, and feminists realized most fully the ideals that inspired President Thomas; at com-

[55] M. Carey Thomas, "The Future of Women in Independent Study and Research," *Publications of the Association of Collegiate Alumnae* (February, 1903), pp. 13–19.

mencement, she reserved her highest praise for the doctoral candidates and the graduates with fellowships for foreign study. To these most select women she offered an austere glory. The woman scholar had to forego marriage; she would never be attracted to a "captain of industry," and she could not do research while running a middle-class home. She had to be free, like a man, to put her work first; she should not have to tend the sick or the aged. Confronted by the "horrible alternative" of marriage or the profession for which she had prepared herself, the woman scholar would choose a spinsterly productivity. The martyr of society, she would enjoy a life of "intellectual renunciation," inspiring young scholars by her costly dedication. If the life was clipped, the guerdon was great. "It is better for the world," President Thomas proclaimed, "for Bryn Mawr to produce one great leader than 100,000 average women."[56]

By 1916, M. Carey Thomas confronted new types of undergraduates: "motor fans," "dancing debs," "life-seeing B— and C students," and flappers. They cut their classes and pronounced their professors bores. She scolded them, but something about these girls, who were eager for life, practical, and energetic, caught her imagination. She recognized another "new woman" in the presumptuous generation which insisted that it learned more on its own than from listening to professors; which had no time to stroll under the maple trees reciting poetry; but which was bent on knowing genetics, engineering, science, and history so as to remold the world. If these girls were not quite her own creation, she took to their cocky pride. She saw no place for the frivolous in "the sacred haunts of the muses," but she was hospitable

56 *Ibid.;* Thomas, "Present Tendencies in Women's College and University Education," pp. 70–75.

to the audacious reformers who were "marching to the rescue" of the world. She replaced the Germanic lecture system, which had inspired her in her youth, with tutorials; and in 1915, over faculty protests, she instituted the Carola Woerishoffer Department of Social Economics and Social Research "in order to afford post-graduate women students an opportunity to obtain preparation for work in social economics." In 1919, she established an experimental school for children, where Bryn Mawr students could observe progressive teaching methods and learn the value of open-air instruction.[57] Her critics sniffed duplicity in her insisting on Bryn Mawr scholarliness while at the same time harboring programs so academically suspect. They failed to see how game she was for anything that would serve "THE CAUSE." Her ideal had always verged on the picaresque; as long as women moved toward victory, they might don any guise. She was ready to back them all—scholars, bridgebuilders, architects, suffragettes, college presidents; they had only to triumph.

As the twentieth century brought new possibilities for women's work in the world, M. Carey Thomas gave her vigorous support to the suffrage, prohibition, and international peace movements. As she traveled across Europe, the Orient, and Africa, collecting objects and curios for the Bryn Mawr Deanery, the idea of the educated woman continued to inspire her to venturesome dreams. In 1921, after having a "vision in the desert" of the possibility of industrial harmony and world peace, she founded Bryn Mawr's Summer School for Women Workers, where women factory workers could receive an education identical with that of the Bryn Mawr undergrad-

[57] M. Carey Thomas, Notes for an address, 1916 (Bryn Mawr College Archives).

uates. As always, President Thomas' creative enthusiasm sprang from the hope that women could tap the "deep sex sympathy" that united them and provide all their sex with "the greatest treasure in the world, a liberal education."[58]

V

Different as these three women were, they had at least a melancholy community: they were all more readily venerated than loved. Men and other women often found them oppressive, and their aspirations made for friction. Thus, Catharine Beecher's three-week visits often seemed long to her hosts, and even longer to their children. In Concord and Boston, Margaret Fuller played the bristling role of an ugly and learned woman; her countrymen paid tribute to her genius, but it was the Italians who first found her *simpatica*.[59] M. Carey Thomas cut her life to suit the angular pattern of her ambition; certain that marriage conflicted with her plans, she made of the pretty, bumptious girl of her youth a huge and formidable presence, a character around whom stories grew.

Their common fate was perhaps the cost of their lonely commitment to the woman that education might create. They lacked the grace of acquiescence: thorny, critical, at odds, they were not typical women. Still, they required that women march to the beat of their drums, and they found an audience for their impassioned criticism. They were disturbed by the conviction that everywhere around them, and perhaps within themselves, life was being

[58] M. Carey Thomas, Address at the opening of the Bryn Mawr School for Women Workers, 1922 (Bryn Mawr College Archives).
[59] Margaret Fuller to Ralph Waldo Emerson, July, 1848 (RWEMA).

wasted. If their programs varied, the differences sprang to a great extent from differences in the periods in which they lived and in the audiences to whom they spoke.

The ideal woman of Catharine Beecher's imagination served a nation where Western settlement, immigrant workers, and new urban wealth threatened the stability of the family. Knowledgeable, energetic, handy, her American housewife managed: she trained her servants but could cope without them; she could nurse, cook, educate, protect, and save. She was master of all the arts her calling required, and, with her many skills and her grave responsibilities, she earned both honor and power. The image was clear, but somehow it failed to satisfy.

Drawing her friends from the professional and merchant classes of the Boston area, Margaret Fuller spoke to women who, like herself, had time to study German, attend lectures, ponder, and converse. Though largely self-educated, they dared to measure their wits against those of their brothers, friends, and husbands; and they made the soul their stalking-ground. "It is difficult for me to feel myself a woman," Caroline Sturgis wrote to Emerson in 1840; "I am such a questioner and feel myself so much more as a soul."[60] To such women, education meant self-discovery and self-expression, and Margaret Fuller tried to provide her friends with talk that would not smell of the schoolroom but would quarry, with unpedantic grace, for the truth itself.

Born two generations later than Catharine Beecher and Margaret Fuller, M. Carey Thomas would find Miss Beecher's program demeaning and Miss Fuller's flimsy. She wanted institutional recognition of women's equality with men, and she was able to use capital accumulated by

[60] Caroline Sturgis to Ralph Waldo Emerson, November, 1840 (RWEMA).

Quaker businessmen like Joseph Taylor and million-
aires like John D. Rockefeller to implement her ideal.
She addressed girls, not women; and this focus on ado-
lescents was suited to the era of the "American girl,"
James's "heiress of all the ages," who was celebrated in
popular magazines throughout the late nineteenth century and who emerged in the twentieth, first as Gibson
girl, then as flapper. M. Carey Thomas spoke effectively
because she talked to the increasing number of indulged
girls who (as she assured them) could get anything they
wanted from their fathers and whose ambitions, like her
own, had only been whetted by privilege. To free their
energies and bolster their pride, she offered them hard
work and an academic degree at which no one could
scoff. She created in the Bryn Mawr graduate a woman
who had mastered a course of study as tough as Harvard's
and who could hold her own against any competitor or
any husband. She thus set out to destroy the very basis of
feminine timidity and endowed her graduates with an
assertive confidence, an inspiring nostalgia, and the conviction that women could do great things.

The arguments of these three women remain curiously
pertinent and disturbing, perhaps because we find in each
some part of our own confusion. Though they wanted a
great deal, their ambitions do not seem strange for their
extravagance so much as for their incompleteness. They
addressed a restlessness not less pervasive for being less
egregious than their own, an unrest only aggravated by
the possibility that the chief problem of the American
woman was that she was spoiled. They themselves knew
at first hand the indulgence of the American male: they
had been petted and made much of by their fathers,
brothers, lovers, and friends. The gallant, extravagant
deference of an Alcott or an Emerson matched for weird-

ness Margaret Fuller's mountainous self-esteem. As M. Carey Thomas bullied, cajoled, and schemed her way to building a great institution, she was served by her father and her uncles, as well as by her superior, President Rhoads. Yet indulgence was not enough, and each tried to construct some ampler stage, where women could move with dignity, assurance, and ease. So by providing domestic know-how, or earnest talk, or the discipline of learning, they attempted to set before their world versions of the creature woman might become.

Fabulous and faintly outlandish, the idols of their imaginings move before us like the distortions of familiar dreams, but with all their lopsidedness they bring the shock of recognition that establishes their viability. For these women provided a peculiarly American escape from the peculiarly American dread of being "stuck" in one job or one place. Conjointly, they added to the live options of later women by making "the feminine" seem legitimately various. So they bequeathed to their successors the nervousness, the risk, and the liberty of having many choices.

I

Catharine Beecher

1. Childhood*

*Catharine Beecher modeled her ideal Christian house-
hold upon that of her childhood and summoned her
readers to recapture the innocence and energy of the
rural past of New England. Her exemplary housewife,
whom she described in numerous best sellers, handily
united the sweetness of her mother, the nervous thrift of
her aunt, and the deftness she had herself displayed when
at sixteen she took over domestically for her bereaved
father. In the following letters, written to piece out Lyman Beecher's "autobiography," she sketched the buoy-
ant and restless household that inspired her long crusade.*

DEAR BROTHER,—The first five years of father's Litchfield
ministry, I think, were probably a period of more unal-
loyed happiness than any in his whole life. Mother enjoyed perfect health, and sympathized thoroughly with
him in all his tastes and employments. The children were
full of health and spirits, under a wise and happy family
government. Aunt Mary spent much of her time with us,
and some of mother's favorite pupils, who had come to
attend Miss Pierce's school, sought a home in our family.
Betsy Burr, an orphan cousin, lived with us like an

* *The Autobiography of Lyman Beecher,* edited by Barbara M.
Cross (Cambridge, Mass.: Harvard University Press, 1961), I, 159–
162, 235–239, abridged.

adopted daughter till her marriage, which took place at our house.

The kitchen department was under the care of the good and affectionate Zillah and Rachel, who came with us from Long Island, and completed the home circle.

Mother was of that easy and gentle temperament that could never very strictly enforce any rules; while father, you know, was never celebrated for his habits of system and order. Of course there was a free and easy way of living, more congenial to liberty and sociality than to conventional rules. As I look back to those days, there is an impression of sunshine, love, and busy activity, without any memory of a jar or cloud.

In about a year or two after father's removal, Grandma Beecher and Aunt Esther gave up the old homestead in New Haven, and the half of the next house to ours on the way to Prospect Hill became their home. To this snug little establishment, so neat and orderly, we children always approached with somewhat of the Oriental feeling that we must put the shoes off our feet, or at least wipe them very clean, to enter such immaculate domains.

There sat Grandma Beecher in her rocking-chair—a neat, precise, upright little lady, with sparkling black eyes, and every thing around her arranged in exactest order, while Aunt Esther watched over and waited upon her with unlimited devotion.

This was the daily resort of father or some of the family, while Aunt Esther came over to our house daily for some errand, or to enjoy a chat with mother.

An important element of father's domestic and literary history was found in the society of Aunt Mary Hubbard and Uncle Samuel Foote. Mother's tastes were rather for subjects of a scientific and metaphysical cast, while Aunt Mary inclined predominantly to polite literature and works of imagination. Each, however, joined with keen relish in the favorite pursuits of the other.

Aunt Mary was a beautiful reader, and I have the most vivid recollection of the impassioned tones in which her favorite authors were given to the family circle. At East Hampton, when I was only eight or nine, my mind was stored with weird tales from Scott's ballads, while the 'Lay of the Last Minstrel' and 'Marmion' were read aloud, mingled with enthusiastic encomiums on favorite passages.

I remember a visit of Uncle Samuel while we lived at East Hampton, in which he brought with him various literary works, and also some of the first numbers of 'Salmagundi,' conducted by Irving and his literary clique, whose career was then just commencing. These papers were read aloud in the family with great enjoyment of their fresh and piquant humor. After we moved to Litchfield, Uncle Samuel came among us, on his return from each voyage, as a sort of brilliant genius of another sphere, bringing gifts and wonders that seemed to wake new faculties in all. Sometimes he came from the shores of Spain, with mementoes of the Alhambra and the ancient Moors; sometimes from Africa, bringing Oriental caps or Moorish slippers; sometimes from South America, with ingots of silver, or strange implements from the tombs of the Incas, or hammocks wrought by the Southern Indian tribes. With these came exciting stories of his adventures, and of the interesting persons of various lands whom he had carried as passengers on his ship on such foreign shores.

He was a man of great practical common sense, united with large ideality, a cultivated taste, and very extensive reading. With this was combined a humorous combativeness, that led him to attack the special theories and prejudices of his friends, sometimes jocosely and sometimes in good earnest.

Of course he and father were in continual good-natured skirmishes, in which all New England peculiarities of theology or of character were held up both in caricature and in sober verity.

I remember long discussions in which he maintained that the Turks were more honest than Christians, bringing very startling facts in evidence. Then I heard his serious tales of Roman Catholic bishops and archbishops he had carried to and from Spain and America, whom he affirmed to be as learned and as truly pious and devoted to the good of men as any Protestant to be found in America. His account of the Jews in Morocco was most curious, their condition appearing, even to his skeptical mind, the strongest verification of Hebrew prophecy. Poor, ignorant, despised, abused in every way, and offered the privileges and dignity of Mussulmen if they would relinquish their faith, they still clung to their sacred books and their despised people with the pertinacity and heroism of martyrs.

The new fields of vision presented by my uncle, the skill and adroitness of his arguments, the array of his facts, combined to tax father's powers to their utmost.

In the literary circle of Litchfield, especially to the female portion, Uncle Samuel appeared as a sort of hero of romance. He spoke French with ease, and made such proficiency in the Spanish tongue that a Spanish gentleman once, after conversing with him, remarked that, were he to meet him in any part of the world, he should know he was born in Castile.

Whenever he came to Litchfield he brought a stock of new books, which he and Aunt Mary read aloud. This was the time when Scott, Byron, Moore, and that great galaxy of contemporary writers were issuing their works at intervals of only a few months, all of which were read and reread in the family circle.

Such a woman as Aunt Mary naturally attracted the attention of the law students, who visited freely in the families of the town. These gentlemen also entered with enthusiasm into her pursuits and tastes, so that the associations of general society were in a measure modified by her unconscious but pervading influence.

Two other persons should be introduced, who, during our whole Litchfield life, were constant visitors or inmates of our family. Mrs. Deveaux was the orphan daughter of a British officer, and the ward of John Murray, one of the oldest and wealthiest families of New York. At fifteen she married Dr. Deveaux, and resided in Camden, South Carolina, till his death, when she returned with her only child Theodosia, and became a resident in Litchfield. Mrs. Deveaux was an indulged child, lively, witty, unreasonable, and a most unmerciful talker. Warm-hearted, intelligent, and very appreciative, she immediately became a great admirer of mother and Aunt Mary. Theodosia was just my age—a bright, gentle, timid girl, with much natural delicacy and common sense. We immediately formed a warm friendship, which was cordially cherished by her mother. Many people regarded Mrs. Deveaux as a rattle and a bore; but mother saw her good qualities, felt a tender sympathy for her and her child, and made them so happy with us that they seemed almost a part of the family. When grown up, Theodosia boarded with us some time, and at last was married at our house. Mrs. Deveaux made every one around her acquainted with all her friends, her surroundings, and her history, and Theodosia was full of narratives of her New York and South Carolina life. Thus we had an outlook into phases of life diverse from ours, which was both instructive and amusing.

*   *   *

DEAR BROTHER,—The year of our great family sorrow brought forth also 'the peaceable fruits of righteousness.' The first event that followed the death of our mother was the removal of Aunt Esther, with her mother, to our house, to take charge of the family. What a sacrifice of personal tastes, ease, and comfort this was to them, can be better appreciated if we consider what was their character, what they gave up, and what they undertook to do.

Grandma Beecher was a fine specimen of the Puritan character of the strictest pattern. She was naturally kind, generous, and sympathizing, as has been seen in her great tenderness for animals; in her wise and patient accommodation to her husband's hypochondriac infirmities; in her generous offer to give up her little patrimony rather than have father, her step-son, taken from college. Conscience was the predominating element in her character. She was strict with herself and strict with all around.

Aunt Esther, her only child, was brought up under the most rigid system of rules, to which she yielded the most exact and scrupulous obedience; and yet, such was her mother's fear that one so good and so bright would 'think more highly of herself than she ought to think,' that the result was most depressing on the character and happiness of the daughter. The habitual sense of her own shortcomings; the dread of any increase of responsibilities; the fear of sinful failure in whatever she should attempt; the quiet life she had led so many years with grandma in the little establishment of bedroom, parlor, and half a kitchen; her habits of extreme neatness and order—all these seemed to forbid even the wish that

Aunt Esther should be asked to assume the management of such a household as ours.

But her love and sympathy overcame all impediments, and very soon grandma's parlor opened from our north entry, her neat carpet, her bright brass andirons, her rocking-chair, her trim, erect figure, with bright black eyes and arched eyebrows, all combining to induce carefulness and quiet around the premises.

Our mother's early training was in the free and easy dominions of General Ward, while Grandma Foote's chief doctrine was that every body, especially children, should do every thing and have every thing they wanted.

At both Nutplains and East Hampton the style of housekeeping was the simplest order, demanding little outlay of time or labor compared with more modern methods. The style of dress for children also required very little expense of material or of time in making. Our mother was gifted with great skill and celerity in all manner of handicraft, and was industrious in the use of time. Thus neither mantua-maker, tailoress, or milliner had ever drawn on the family treasury.

But kind, anxious, economical Aunt Esther had no gift in this line. As a close economist, as an accomplished cook, as systematic, orderly, and neat in all family arrangements, none could excel her, but with scissors and needle she felt helpless and less than nothing; so that, although she could patch and darn respectably, and grandma could knit and mend stockings, the preparation of wardrobes for the eight children rose before her as a mountain of difficulty. It was here that father's good sense, quick discernment, and tender sympathy wisely intervened. He gently and tenderly made me understand the great kindness of grandma and Aunt Esther in giving up their own quiet and comfort to take care of us; he awakened my sympathy for Aunt Esther in her new and difficult position; he stimulated my generous ambition to supply my mother's place in the care of the younger children, especially in the department in which he assured me he knew I would excel, and that was where Aunt Esther most needed help.

Happily, our mother's skill in household handicraft was bequeathed in some good measure to her daughters; and thus stimulated, I, for the first time, undertook all the labor of cutting, fitting, and making all the clothing of the children, as well as my own. So also, under Aunt Esther's careful training, Mary and I were initiated into all the arts of kitchen labor, cheered and animated by the consciousness that it comforted father and relieved Aunt Esther.

There are some who control the young in such a way as to make them feel that all they do is nothing more than what they ought to do, and usually considerably less. Others have the happy faculty, which our father possessed in a remarkable degree, of discovering and rejoicing over unexpected excellence in character and conduct. He not only felt pleased and grateful when kindnesses were done to him and his, but he had the *gift of expression*. He not only discovered and appreciated all that was good in character and conduct, but he made known his pleased approval.

Oil and water were not more opposite than the habits of father and Aunt Esther, and yet they flowed along together in all the antagonisms of daily life without jar or friction. All Aunt Esther's rules and improvements were admired and commended, and, though often overridden, the contrite confession or droll excuse always brought a forgiving smile. Indeed, it was father's constant boast to Aunt Esther that, *naturally,* he was a man possessing great neatness, order, and system; that the only difficulty was, they were all *inside,* and that it was Aunt Esther's special mission to bring them out. And he had a triumphant way of taking her around, whenever he arranged his outdoor implements or indoor surroundings in any respectable order, to *prove* to her that it was his *nature* to be orderly and careful.

In this new administration the older children were brought in as co-laborers, inspired by the sympathetic, grateful, and appreciative sentiments father communicated to the family. All the children were in habits of prompt obedience, were healthful, cheerful, and full of activity. With these busy workers around, and Aunt Esther to lead, every room, from garret to cellar, was put in neat and regular trim; every basket, bundle, box, and bag overhauled, and every patch, remnant, and shred laid out smooth, sorted, and rolled, folded, or arranged in perfect order; all aged garments were mended to the last extremity of endurance; pegs and hooks were put in position, where coats, pantaloons, jackets, hats, caps, bonnets, shawls, and cloaks were to conform to the rule, 'a place for every thing, and every thing in its place.' The barn, the garden, and the orchard were the only cities of refuge from this inflexible rule.

The special object of nightmare dread to Aunt Esther was *debt.* The fear that under her administration the expenditures would exceed the salary could be relieved by no possible calculations; and so we learned, on every hand, rules of the closest economy and calculation. We were saved, however, from all uncomfortable retrenchments by the abundance of gifts from generous and sympathizing friends and parishioners. So we gained the benefits without the evils. But, in spite of all, Aunt Esther was burdened with ceaseless anxiety. The responsibility of providing for the family, the care of eight young children as to wardrobe, health, and behavior, and the thousand and one responsibilities that rested upon one so exact, so conscientious, and so self-distrustful, was a burden too great for her to bear, and we all felt anxious and troubled to see her so burdened; yet she rarely complained, seldom found fault, and never scolded. Whenever any thing went wrong, or the children misbehaved, grandma's black eyes peered over her spectacles like two cold stars, and Aunt Esther sighed, and looked discouraged and sad.

The experience of this year of our family history was similar to that of a landscape in sunshine suddenly overcast with heavy clouds. The gentle, contented, smiling, healthful mother was gone, and the sunlight of our home departed with her to return no more.

In noticing the many alleviating blessings of this period of sorrow, one may be noticed as presenting a cheering feature of the pastoral relation in the universal and tender sympathy of the parish, manifested in many ways. Our mother was but little known by personal acquaintance in the parish; but her reputation as a woman of talent and culture, her diligent devotion to her numerous family, the sweet and modest expression of her countenance in church, and the gentle blush that always appeared whenever she was addressed, awakened a universal and tender interest, and her untimely death called forth unexpected and universal sorrow and sympathy. This was manifested in many kindnesses offered, especially in an influx of presents and offers of aid from all classes. The family were provided with complete suits of mourning as gifts from one friend or another, while almost daily some token of kindness and sympathy arrived.

The most remarkable and unique of these demonstrations was what in New England is called the *minister's wood-spell*, when, by previous notice, on some bright winter day, every person in the parish who chooses to do so sends a sled load of wood as a present to the pastor. On this occasion we were previously notified that the accustomed treat of dough-nuts and loaf-cake, cider and flip, must be on a much larger scale than common.

With father's rejoicing approval, I was allowed to take both the responsibility and the labor of this whole occasion, with Aunt Esther as my guide, and the younger children as my helpers, and for nearly a week our kitchen was busy as an ant-hill. For preliminaries, the fat was to be prepared to boil the dough-nuts, the spices to be pounded, the sugar to be rolled, the flour to be sifted, and the materials for beer for the flip to be collected. Next came the brewing, on a scale of grandeur befitting the occasion. Then the cake was duly made, and placed in large stone pots or earthen jars set around the kitchen fire, and duly turned and tended till the proper lightness was detected. Lastly came the baking of the loaves and the boiling of the dough-nuts; and were I to tell the number of loaves I put into and took out of the oven, and the bushels of dough-nuts I boiled over the kitchen fire, I fear my credit for veracity would be endangered. Certainly our kitchen, store-room, and pantry were a sight to behold, calling in admiring visitors, while my success was the matter of universal gratulation.

When the auspicious day arrived, the snow was thick, smooth, and well packed for the occasion; the sun shone through a sharp, dry, and frosty air; and the whole town was astir. Toward the middle of the afternoon, runners arrived with news of the gathering squadrons—Mount Tom was coming with all its farmers; Bradleyville also; Chestnut Hill, and the North and the South settlements; while the "town hill" gentry were on the *qui vive* to hunt up every sled and yoke of oxen not employed by their owners. Before sundown the yard, street, and the lower rooms of our house were swarming with cheerful faces. Father was ready with his cordial greetings, adroit in detecting and admiring the special merits of every load as it arrived. The kind farmers wanted to see all the children, and we were busy as bees in waiting on them. The boys heated the flip-irons, and passed around the cider and flip, while Aunt Esther and the daughters were as busy in serving the dough-nuts, cake, and cheese. And such a mountainous wood-pile as arose in our yard never before was seen in ministerial domains!

It needed all these alleviations, and more also, to sustain father under the heavy pressure that rested on his spirits. He rarely spoke of the loss that wrung his brave, yet fainting heart, that strove to keep up strength and courage by counting its blessings instead of its pains. But years after, one day, pointing to a large basket, he said, 'Henry, there are the sermons I wrote the year after your mother died, and there is not one of them good for any thing!'

Never do the reverses of life so unman the soul as on the festivals that bring together a family after its golden circle is broken. At the first Thanksgiving Day after mother died we assembled round the table, all dressed in our newly-finished suits, the house all in perfect order, our store-room filled with abundance of presents, our table loaded with the nicest specimens of culinary skill. When all were in order, and father was to 'ask the blessing,' we waited long in silence, while the great tears stole down his cheeks amid the sighs and tears of all around. Then followed, in a calm, subdued voice, such an offering of patient, peaceful thankfulness and love, as if the gentle spirit we mourned was near, shedding peace and comfort from her wings.

2. The Hartford Female Seminary*

When she was seventy-four, Catharine Beecher summed up her life in a rambling chronicle of her educational causes and wars. Her first school, the Hartford Female Seminary, established her reputation, and she was always ready to describe her pedagogical successes there. She ran the school for seven years, interrupting her work only when nervous exhaustion forced her to take the "water cure," thus giving her sister and other subordinate teachers a respite from her imperious rule. The following selection describes the educational experiments of the school.

The art of composition has seldom been made the subject of *instruction* in schools, and the success of classes under the care of my sister, Mrs. Stowe, was so remarkable that the methods pursued are worthy of notice.

The first exercise was to provide a stock of *words,* by reading a short, classical story, explaining the meaning of every new or difficult word, and then requiring the pupils to use these words as they wrote the story on a slate, we having already explained and illustrated on the blackboard the use of capitals, punctuation, and paragraphing. Then these slates were corrected by the teacher and

* Catharine E. Beecher, *Educational Reminiscences and Suggestions* (New York: J. B. Ford and Co., 1874), pp. 38–46, abridged.

assistant pupils, and, next day, the composition was neatly copied, folded properly, and brought to the teacher. These exercises were to be constantly varied as to the authors and subjects selected, and all but copying was to be done in the Composition Room.

Next, an extract from some classic writer was read over twice, and then the pupils wrote the principal words in this passage, their meaning being first explained. Then the passage was read a third time, and the pupils were required to write on their slates the same passages as nearly as remembered, introducing all the words given them. This also was criticised and corrected by the teacher and assistant pupils, to be neatly copied and returned next day. The teacher would daily select passages from a variety of standard classic writers, point out the peculiarity of style in each; while the pupils, by thus imitating various authors, gradually acquired both a large stock of words and facility in varied modes of expression and style of writing.

Next was taught *methodical arrangement*. This the teacher first explained and illustrated by a general outline of an article, followed by the reading of it, thus analyzed. Then the pupils copied on slates, from dictation, this skeleton or analysis, and were required to fill it out and bring it next day, having heard the piece read the second and perhaps the third time in the class-room.

Next, the teacher selected a subject and proposed questions to excite inquiry and discussion. Then, she gave her own views on the subject, and the way she would prepare her outline or skeleton. Then the pupils were required each to prepare a skeleton, which was duly criticised, and next day it was to be filled out by the class and presented for correction and criticism. This last exercise was often repeated.

Next was taught the use of *poetic language,* by first instructing in the use of poetic feet and rhymes, and then requiring a short piece of poetry to be turned to prose, and then, without committing to memory, to change the prose back to poetry.

To mature and advanced pupils, *unity* and *method* were taught, by giving some essay with several chapters (for example, one of Macaulay's essays), and then requiring a written statement of the plan of the whole; then, an analysis of each chapter; then, of each paragraph, and its connexion with the whole.

When this was all completed, the pupil was supposed to be prepared to write a composition.

This method was so interesting that the composition hour was looked forward to as the pleasantest part of school duty; and the results were such as, on any other plan, would seem incredible in pupils of such immaturity, were the method pursued unknown. Of course, in this, as in all other branches, success depends to a large extent on the qualifications of the teacher, and the power of *exciting interest* in the pupils.

Another important particular was the *exact and thorough* knowledge gained by *repetitions* of lessons and general examinations. When any kind of knowledge is gained with little interest and in an indistinct way, it soon fades from the memory, and thus many pupils lose nearly as fast as they gain. Our method was a weekly review, with the anticipation of a fortnight public examination before visitors at the close of each term. And if laggards were found in any class, they were liable to be detained after school and drilled till the neglected lesson was perfect. Our aim was to have all so perfect in daily lessons that the weeks of examination would not be periods of unusual exertion except to the dull or the negligent, who were then special objects of attention from the chief teachers. Indeed, it was the rule to give most care and labor to the weaker lambs of the fold, whatever were the causes of their deficiencies. It is too often the case that, for the credit of the school or the pleasure of teaching the brightest and best, this rule is reversed.

The attempt to remedy physical defects came about in this manner: An English lady of fine person and manner came to us as a teacher of what then had no name, but now would be called *Calisthenics*. She gave a large number of the exercises that are in my work on *Physiology and Calisthenics,* published by the Harpers, and narrated how she had cured deformities in others by her methods. What interested us most was her assurance that, until maturity she had a curvature of the spine that was a sad deformity, being what was called a humpback, and yet there she was, a model of fine proportion and gracefulness. The whole school took lessons of her, and I added others; and though the results were not conspicuous, they convinced me that far more might be done in this direction than was ever imagined or would be credited without ocular demonstration. From this came the system of Calisthenics which I invented, which spread all over the country, and which Dio Lewis, courteously giving me due credit, modified and made additions to, some of which I deem not improvements but objectionable, for reasons stated elsewhere.

3. The Education of Female Teachers*

By 1835, Catharine Beecher was so well known that the American Lyceum invited her to deliver an address on the education of women teachers. The speech, published "at the desire of a meeting of Ladies in New York" and reprinted, in part, below, outlined several projects that her American Women's Educational Association later sponsored, such as the endowment of female normal schools and the enlistment of the benevolence of Eastern ladies to redeem the nation. Like other contemporary educationists, she held European models reproachfully before her republican fellows.

Woman, whatever are her relations in life, is necessarily the guardian of the nursery, the companion of childhood, and the constant model of imitation. It is her hand that first stamps impressions on the immortal spirit, that must remain forever. And what demands such discretion, such energy, such patience, such tenderness, love, and wisdom, such perspicacity to discern, such versatility to modify, such efficiency to execute, such firmness to persevere, as the government and education of all the various characters and tempers that meet in the nursery and school-room? Woman also is the presiding genius who must regulate all those thousand minutiæ of domestic business,

* Catharine E. Beecher, *An Essay on the Education of Female Teachers* (New York: Van Nostrand and Dwight, 1835), abridged.

that demand habits of industry, order, neatness, punctuality, and constant care. And it is for such varied duties that woman is to be trained. For this her warm sympathies, her lively imagination, her ready invention, her quick perceptions, all need to be cherished and improved; while at the same time those more foreign habits, of patient attention, calm judgment, steady efficiency, and habitual self-control, must be induced and sustained.

Is a weak, undisciplined, unregulated mind, fitted to encounter the responsibility, weariness, and watching of the nursery; to bear the incessant care and perplexity of governing young children; to accommodate with kindness and patience to the peculiarities and frailties of a husband; to control the indolence, waywardness, and neglect of servants; and to regulate all the variety of domestic cares? The superficial accomplishments of former periods were of little avail to fit a woman for such arduous duties; and for this reason it is, that as society has advanced in all other improvements, the course of female education has been gradually changing, and some portion of that mental discipline, once exclusively reserved for the other sex, is beginning to exert its invigorating influence upon the female character. At the same time the taste of the age is altered; and, instead of the fainting, weeping, vapid, pretty play-thing, once the model of female loveliness, those qualities of the head and heart that best qualify a woman for her duties, are demanded and admired.

None will deny the importance of having females properly fitted for their peculiar duties; and yet few are aware how much influence a teacher may exert in accomplishing this object. School is generally considered as a place where children are sent, not to form their habits, opinions, and character, but simply to learn from books.

And yet, whatever may be the opinion of teachers and parents, children do, to a very great extent, form their character under influences bearing upon them at school. They are proverbially creatures of imitation, and accessible to powerful influences. Six hours every day are spent with teachers, whom they usually love and respect, and whose sentiments and opinions, in one way or another, they constantly discover. They are at the same time associated with companions of all varieties of temper, character, and habit. Is it possible that this can exist without involving constant and powerful influences, either good or bad? The simple fact that a teacher succeeds in making a child habitually accurate and thorough in all the lessons of school, may induce mental habits that will have a controlling influence through life. If the government of schools be so administered as to induce habits of cheerful and implicit obedience, if punctuality, neatness, and order in all school employments are preserved for a course of years, it must have some influence in forming useful habits. On the contrary, if a child is tolerated in disobedience and neglect, if school duties are performed in a careless, irregular, and deficient manner, pernicious habits may be formed that will operate disastrously through life. It is true that mismanagement and indulgence at home may counteract all the good influences of school; and the faithful discharge of parental duty may counteract, to some extent, the bad influences of school: but this does not lessen the force of these considerations.

Nor is the course of study and mental discipline of inferior consequence. The mere committing to memory of the facts contained in books, is but a small portion of education. Certain portions of time should be devoted to fitting a woman for her practical duties: such, for ex-

ample, as needlework. Other pursuits are designed for
the cultivation of certain mental faculties, such as *attention, perseverance,* and *accuracy*. This, for example, is
the influence of the study of the mathematics; while the
conversation and efforts of a teacher, directed to this end,
may induce habits of investigation and correct reasoning,
not to be secured by any other method. Other pursuits
are designed to cultivate the taste and imagination:
such as rhetoric, poetry, and other branches of polite literature. Some studies are fitted to form correct moral
principles, and strengthen religious obligation: such as
mental and moral philosophy, the study of the evidences
of Christianity, the study of the Bible, and of collateral
subjects. Other studies are designed to store the mind
with useful knowledge: such, for example, as geography,
history, and the natural sciences. The proper selection
and due proportion of these various pursuits, will have
a decided influence in forming the mental habits and
general character of the pupils.

When it is asserted that it is of more consequence that
women be educated to be virtuous, useful, and pious,
than that they become learned and accomplished, every
one assents to the truth of the position. When it is said
that it is the most important and most difficult duty of
parents and teachers, to form the moral character, the
principles and habits of children, no one will dissent. All
allow it to be a labor demanding great watchfulness,
great wisdom, and constant perseverance and care. For
what comfort would parents find in the assurance, that
their children are intelligent, learned, and accomplished,
if all is to be perverted by indolence, vice, and irreligion?
And what is the benefit to society, in increasing the
power of intellect and learning, if they only add to the
evils of contaminating example and ruinous vice? The

necessity of *virtuous* intelligence in the mass of the community is peculiarly felt in a form of government like ours, where the people are not held in restraint by physical force, as in despotic governments, but where, if they do not voluntarily submit to the restraints of virtue and religion, they must inevitably run loose to wild misrule, anarchy, and crime. For a nation to be virtuous and religious, the females of that nation must be deeply imbued with these principles: for just as the wives and mothers sink or rise in the scale of virtue, intelligence, and piety, the husbands and the sons will rise or fall. These positions scarce any intelligent person will deny: so that it may be set down as one of the current truisms of society, that the formation of the moral and religious principles and habits is the most important part of education, even in reference to this life alone. To this is added the profession of all who reverence Christianity, that the interests of an immortal state of being are equally suspended on the same results.

In regard to education, the world is now making experiments, such as were never made before. Man is demanding disenthralment, alike from physical force, and intellectual slavery; and, by a slow and secret process, one nation after another is advancing in a sure, though silent progress. Man is bursting the chains of slavery, and the bonds of intellectual subserviency; and is learning to think, and reason, and act for himself. And the great crisis is hastening on, when it shall be decided whether disenthralled intellect and liberty shall voluntarily submit to the laws of virtue and of Heaven, or run wild to insubordination, anarchy, and crime. The great questions pending before the world, are simply these: are liberty and intelligence, without the restraints of a moral and religious education, a blessing, or a curse? Without moral and religious restraints, is it best for man to receive the gift of liberty and intelligence, or to remain coerced by physical force, and the restraints of opinions and customs not his own?

The master-spirits of the age are watching the developments as they rise, and making their records for the instruction of mankind.

And what results are already gained? In England, the experiment has been made by the sceptical Brougham; and, at great expense, knowledge has gone forth with increasing liberty, and all who have witnessed the results are coming to the conviction, that increase of knowledge, without moral and religious influence, is only increase of vice and discontent. And what are the results of the experiment in France? The statistics of education show, that the best educated departments are the most vicious, and the most ignorant are the freest from crime. And, in that country, where the national representatives once declared that Christianity should be banished, and the Bible burnt, and the Sabbath annihilated, we now find its most distinguished statesmen and citizens uniting in the public declaration, that moral and religious education must be the foundation of national instruction. Victor Cousin, one of the most distinguished philosophers of the age, and appointed by the King of France to examine the various systems of education in Europe, has reported, as the result of his investigations, that education is a blessing, just in proportion as it is founded on moral and religious principles.

Look, again, at Prussia! with its liberal and patriotic monarch, with a system of education unequalled in the records of time, requiring by law that all the children in the nation be sent to school, from the first day they are seven years of age, till the last day they are fourteen, with a regular course of literary and scientific instruction, instituted for every school, and every teacher required to spend three years in preparing for such duties; while, on an average, one teacher is furnished for every ten pupils through the nation. The effects of merely intellectual culture soon convinced the monarch and his counsellors that moral and religious instruction must be the basis of all their efforts; and now the Bible is placed in every school, and every teacher is required to spend from one to two hours each day, in giving and enforcing instruction in all the duties of man towards his Creator, towards constituted authorities, and towards his fellow-men.

And what is the experience of our own country? Those portions of the nation, most distinguished for the general diffusion of education, are those in which moral and religious influences have been most extensively introduced into schools, and have pervaded all the institutions of society. But, in those portions of our country the increase and jealousy of religious sects, and other combining causes, have had an influence in banishing the Bible, and moral and religious influence, more and more from public schools. And now we hear the widely extended complaint, that common schools are dangerous places for children; while parents, who are most regardful of the moral influences exerted upon their children, are more and more withdrawing them from what they deem such contaminating influence.

What patriot, what philanthropist, what Christian, does not see that all that is sacred and dear in home, and country, and liberty, and religion, call upon him to waken every energy, and put forth every effort?

Does the heart fail, and the courage sink, at the magnitude of the work, and the apparent destitution of means? We have the means—we have the power. There is wealth enough, and benevolence enough, and self-denying laborers enough. Nothing is wanting but a knowledge of our danger, our duty, and our means, and a willing mind in exerting our energies. Our difficulties and danger have been briefly noticed. It is the object of this essay to point out one important measure in the system of means that must be employed.

Men of patriotism and benevolence can commence by endowing two or three seminaries for female teachers in the most important stations in the nation, while to each of these seminaries shall be attached a model school, supported by the children of the place where it is located. In these seminaries can be collected those who have the highest estimate of the value of moral and religious influence, and the most talents and experience for both intellectual and moral education.

When these teachers shall have succeeded in training classes of teachers on the best system their united wisdom can devise, there will be instructors prepared for other seminaries for teachers, to be organized and conducted on the same plan; and thus a regular and systematic course of education can be disseminated through the nation.

And, as a system of right moral and religious education gains its appropriate influence, as women are more and more educated to understand and value the importance of their influence in society, and their peculiar duties, more young females will pursue their education with the expectation that, unless paramount private duties forbid, they are to employ their time and talents in the duties of a teacher, until they assume the responsibilities of domestic life. Females will cease to feel that they are educated just to enjoy themselves in future life, and realize the obligations imposed by Heaven to live to do good. And, when females are educated as they ought to be, every woman at the close of her school education, will be well qualified to act as a teacher.

4. Teachers to the West*

*In 1846, Catharine Beecher helped establish the Board of
National Popular Education to raise funds and enlist
teachers for schools in the West and South. She soon
quarreled with Governor William Slade, head of the or-
ganization, and eventually founded a rival group of her
own. At women's meetings in Eastern cities, she read
letters like the following, which were written to her by
teachers in the West. The letters reveal the religious commitment and the hygienic aims of these gallant and di-
dactic pioneers.*

I arrived here the 17th of January, and opened school in
a small log house. I now have forty-five pupils, one-half
of whom are boys, and some of them grown up. They all
seem anxious to please me, and I find no difficulty in
governing them.

The inhabitants here are chiefly from North Carolina,
Tennessee, and Germany. All are farmers, and their chief
object is to make money. They seem desirous to have
their children educated, but they differed so much about
almost everything, that they could not build a school-
house. I was told, also, when I came that they would not
pay a teacher for more than three months in a year. At
first they were very suspicious, and watched me narrowly;
but, through the blessing of my Heavenly Father, I have

* Catharine E. Beecher, *Educational Reminiscences and Suggestions* (New York: J. B. Ford and Co., 1874), pp. 121–125.

gained their good will and confidence, so that they have built me a good frame school-house, with writing-desks and a black-board, and promise to support me all the year round.

I commence school every day with reading the Bible and prayer; this was new to them, but they made no objections. The people here spend Sunday in hunting, fishing, and visiting. I have commenced a Sabbath-school and invited the parents to come with their children. They seem much pleased, and many come three and four miles. They never heard of a Sunday-school before. Last Sunday there were fifty present, and I proposed that we should have a Bible-class for the men, and that Mr.—, a professor of religion near this place, should take charge of it, while I attended to the women and children. There being no church nearer than seven miles, the people think it too much trouble to go to it. I have persuaded them to invite the nearest clergyman to preach in my school-house next Sunday.

My greatest trials here are the want of religious privileges, the difficulty of sending to the distant post-office, the entire want of social sympathy, and the manner in which I am obliged to live. I board where there are eight children and the parents, and only two rooms in the house. I must do as the family do about washing, as there is but one basin and no place to go to wash but out the door. I have not enjoyed the luxury of either lamp or candle, their only light being a cup of grease with a rag for a wick. Evening is my only time to write, but this kind of light makes such a disagreeable smoke and smell I cannot bear it, and do without light except the fire. I occupy a room with three of the children and a niece who boards here. The other room serves as a kitchen, parlor, and bedroom for the rest of the family.

I have read your *Domestic Economy* through to the family, one chapter a day. They like it, and have adopted some of your suggestions in regard both to *order* and to *health*. They used to drink coffee three times a day. Now they use it only once a day. Their bread used to be heavy and half-baked, but I made yeast by the receipt in your book, and thus made some good bread. They were much pleased with it, and I have made such ever since.

The people here are *very* ignorant; very few of them can either read or write, but they wish to have their children taught. They spend Sunday in visiting and idleness, and the fact that I kept Sunday-school for them without pay convinced them that my real object was to do good. The people in the settlements around are anxious to have more of the teachers come out. They have sent for Miss H., who came out with me, but she was engaged. I was sorry, as it would have been a comfort to have had one friend within reaching distance.

When I came here I intended to stay only one term; but the people urged me so much to remain, and have done so much in building me a school-house, that I concluded to stay longer. I did not leave my home to seek pleasure, wealth, or fame, and I do believe my Heavenly Father will bless my labors here, even if I never see the fruit. The people seem to like me, say their children never behaved so well before, were present at my examination, and like the Eastern way of keeping school.

EXTRACT OF ANOTHER LETTER FROM THE SAME

Your kind letter was received last Thursday, and would have been immediately answered, but I was sent for to visit a sick child. The parents, being Catholic, were much alarmed lest it should die unbaptized. I explained as well as I could the nature and object of baptism, succeeded in quieting their fears, and, as they urged it, I staid all night in the cabin, with only one room, holding nine grown persons besides two children and the sick infant. There was no window, and they kept both doors shut till I persuaded them to leave a small opening to one door. In the morning I walked through the wet prairie and thus took a heavy cold, and for three weeks have been unable to use my eyes.

As soon as I could I took the draft you sent me to the nearest large town and purchased the articles you directed. Ever since I have enjoyed the luxury of bathing and candlelight, and, with my screen, I can be alone at least in a corner. I can never sufficiently thank you for your kindness in thus adding to my comfort and usefulness in a strange land. I am much pleased at the prospect of the books you have sent to me, and the children are highly delighted. Many of my scholars are now sick, and my own health is not so good as it was, as I have watched a good deal with my scholars who were sick of the scarlet and winter fevers. There is a broad field of usefulness here, large enough for all who wish to come. I have never regretted that I came, and if I am made the instrument of bringing *only one* to the knowledge of the truth, I shall be amply repaid for the sacrifices I have made in this noble cause.

5. The Christian Family*

Written with her sister Harriet Beecher Stowe, The
American Woman's Home *expanded Catharine Beecher's many books of counsel for the housewife. The fron-
tispiece (see page 80) renders the iconography of wife-
and-mother which she worked so hard to establish. Save
for the little mother-in-the-making on the floor with her
doll, the group focuses on the mother's face and the book
she is holding; idle and eclipsed, husband, boy, and
grandfather form a halo around the lighted face of the
woman. The table of contents underlines the wide-
ranging duties of women. There are chapters on "Ventilation," "Home Decoration," "Health of Mind," "Care
of Infants," "Care of the Aged," "Early Rising" (a "virtue peculiarly American and democratic"), and "Earth-
Closets."*

It is the aim of this volume to elevate both the honor
and the remuneration of all employments that sustain
the many difficult and varied duties of the family state,
and thus to render each department of woman's profession as much desired and respected as are the most
honored professions of men.

What, then, is the end designed by the family state
which Jesus Christ came into this world to secure?

* Catharine E. Beecher and Harriet Beecher Stowe, *The American
Woman's Home* (New York: J. B. Ford and Co., 1869), Chaps. 1, 22,
abridged.

It is to provide for the training of our race to the highest possible intelligence, virtue, and happiness, by means of the self-sacrificing labors of the wise and good, and this with chief reference to a future immortal existence.

The distinctive feature of the family is self-sacrificing labor of the stronger and wiser members to raise the weaker and more ignorant to equal advantages. The father undergoes toil and self-denial to provide a home, and then the mother becomes a self-sacrificing laborer to train its inmates. The useless, troublesome infant is served in the humblest offices; while both parents unite in training it to an equality with themselves in every advantage. Soon the older children become helpers to raise the younger to a level with their own. When any are sick, those who are well become self-sacrificing ministers. When the parents are old and useless, the children become their self-sacrificing servants.

Thus the discipline of the family state is one of daily self-devotion of the stronger and wiser to elevate and support the weaker members. Nothing could be more contrary to its first principles than for the older and more capable children to combine to secure to themselves the highest advantages, enforcing the drudgeries on the younger, at the sacrifice of their equal culture.

Jesus Christ came to teach the fatherhood of God and consequent brotherhood of man. He came as the "first-born Son" of God and the Elder Brother of man, to teach by example the self-sacrifice by which the great family of man is to be raised to equality of advantages as children of God. For this end, he "humbled himself" from the highest to the lowest place. He chose for his birthplace the most despised village; for his parents the lowest in rank; for his trade, to labor with his hands as a carpenter, being "subject to his parents" thirty years. And, what is very significant, his trade was that which prepares the family home, as if he would teach that the great duty of man is labor—to provide for and train weak and ignorant creatures. Jesus Christ worked with his hands nearly thirty years, and preached less than three. And he taught that his kingdom is exactly opposite to that of the world, where all are striving for the highest positions. "Whoso will be great shall be your minister, and whoso will be chiefest shall be servant of all."

The family state then, is the aptest earthly illustration of the heavenly kingdom, and in it woman is its chief minister. Her great mission is self-denial, in training its members to self-sacrificing labors for the ignorant and weak: if not her own children, then the neglected children of her Father in heaven. She is to rear all under her care to lay up treasures, not on earth, but in heaven. All the pleasures of this life end here; but those who train immortal minds are to reap the fruit of their labor through eternal ages.

To man is appointed the out-door labor—to till the earth, dig the mines, toil in the foundries, traverse the ocean, transport merchandise, labor in manufactories, construct houses, conduct civil, municipal and state affairs, and all the heavy work, which, most of the day, excludes him from the comforts of a home. But the great stimulus to all these toils, implanted in the heart of every true man, is the desire for a home of his own, and the hopes of paternity. Every man who truly lives for immortality responds to the beatitude, "Children are a heritage from the Lord: blessed is the man that hath his quiver full of them!" The more a father and mother live under the influence of that "immortality which Christ hath brought to light," the more is the blessedness of rearing a family understood and appreciated. Every child

trained aright is to dwell forever in exalted bliss with
those that gave it life and trained it for heaven.

The blessed privileges of the family state are not confined to those who rear children of their own. Any woman who can earn a livelihood, as every woman should
be trained to do, can take a properly qualified female
associate, and institute a family of her own, receiving to
its heavenly influences the orphan, the sick, the homeless,
and the sinful, and by motherly devotion train them to
follow the self-denying example of Christ, in educating
his earthly children for true happiness in this life and for
his eternal home.

And such is the blessedness of aiding to sustain a truly
Christian home, that no one comes so near the pattern
of the All-perfect One as those who might hold what men
call a higher place, and yet humble themselves to the
lowest in order to aid in training the young, "not as men-
pleasers, but as servants to Christ, with good-will doing
service as to the Lord, and not to men." Such are preparing for high places in the kingdom of heaven. "Whoso-
ever will be chiefest among you, let him be your servant."

It is often the case that the true humility of Christ is
not understood. It was not in having a low opinion of his
own character and claims, but it was in taking a low
place in order to raise others to a higher. The worldling
seeks to raise himself and family to an equality with
others, or, if possible, a superiority to them. The true fol-
lower of Christ comes down in order to elevate others.

The maxims and institutions of this world have ever
been antagonistic to the teachings and example of Jesus
Christ. Men toil for wealth, honor, and power, not as
means for raising others to an equality with themselves,
but mainly for earthly, selfish advantages. Although the
experience of this life shows that children brought up to

labor have the fairest chance for a virtuous and prosperous life, and for hope of future eternal blessedness, yet it is the aim of most parents who can do so, to lay up wealth that their children need not labor with the hands as Christ did. And although exhorted by our Lord not to lay up treasure on earth, but rather the imperishable riches which are gained in toiling to train the ignorant and reform the sinful, as yet a large portion of the professed followers of Christ, like his first disciples, are "slow of heart to believe."

Not less have the sacred ministries of the family state been undervalued and warred upon in other directions; for example, the Romish Church has made celibacy a prime virtue, and given its highest honors to those who forsake the family state as ordained by God. Thus came great communities of monks and nuns, shut out from the love and labors of a Christian home; thus, also, came the monkish systems of education, collecting the young in great establishments away from the watch and care of parents, and the healthful and self-sacrificing labors of a home. Thus both religion and education have conspired to degrade the family state.

Still more have civil laws and social customs been opposed to the principles of Jesus Christ. It has ever been assumed that the learned, the rich, and the powerful are not to labor with the hands, as Christ did, and as Paul did when he would "not eat any man's bread for naught, but wrought with labor, not because we have not power" [to live without hand-work,] "but to make ourselves an example." (2 Thess. 3.)

Instead of this, manual labor has been made dishonorable and unrefined by being forced on the ignorant and poor. Especially has the most important of all hand-labor, that which sustains the family, been thus disgraced; so that to nurse young children, and provide the food of a family by labor, is deemed the lowest of all positions in honor and profit, and the last resort of poverty. And so our Lord, who himself took the form of a servant, teaches, "How hardly shall they that have riches enter the kingdom of heaven!"—that kingdom in which all are toiling to raise the weak, ignorant, and sinful to such equality with themselves as the children of a loving family enjoy. One mode in which riches have led to antagonism with the true end of the family state is in the style of living, by which the hand-labor, most important to health, comfort, and beauty, is confined to the most ignorant and neglected members of society, without any effort being made to raise them to equal advantages with the wise and cultivated.

And, the higher civilization has advanced, the more have children been trained to feel that to labor, as did Christ and Paul, is disgraceful, and to be made the portion of a degraded class. Children of the rich grow up with the feeling that servants are to work for them, and they themselves are not to work. To the minds of most children and servants, "to be a lady," is almost synonymous with "to be waited on, and do no work." It is the earnest desire of the authors of this volume to make plain the falsity of this growing popular feeling, and to show how much happier and more efficient family life will become when it is strengthened, sustained, and adorned by family work.

THE MANAGEMENT OF YOUNG CHILDREN

There is probably no practice more deleterious, than that of allowing children to eat at short intervals, through the day. As the stomach is thus kept constantly at work, with no time for repose, its functions are deranged, and a weak or disordered stomach is the frequent result. Children should be required to keep cakes, nuts, and other good things, which should be sparingly given, till just before a meal, and then they will form a part of their regular supply. This is better than to wait till after their hunger is satisfied by food, when they will eat the niceties merely to gratify the palate, and thus overload the stomach and interrupt digestion.

In regard to the intellectual training of young children, some modification in the common practice is necessary, with reference to their physical well-being. More care is needful, in providing *well-ventilated* school-rooms, and in securing more time for sports in the open air, during school hours. It is very important to most mothers that their young children should be removed from their care during certain school hours; and it is very useful for quite young children, to be subjected to the discipline of a school, and to intercourse with other children of their own age. And, with a suitable teacher, it is no matter how early children are sent to school, provided their health is not endangered by impure air, too much confinement, and too great mental stimulus, which is the chief danger of the present age.

In regard to the formation of the moral character, it has been too much the case that the discipline of the nursery has consisted of disconnected efforts to make children either do, or refrain from doing, certain particular acts. Do this, and be rewarded; do that, and be punished; is the ordinary routine of family government.

But children can be very early taught that their happiness, both now and hereafter, depends on the formation of *habits* of submission, self-denial, and benevolence. And all the discipline of the nursery can be conducted by parents, not only with this general aim in their own minds, but also with the same object daily set before the minds of the children. Whenever their wishes are crossed, or their wills subdued, they can be taught that all this is done, not merely to please the parent, or to secure some good to themselves or to others; but as a part of that merciful training which is designed to form such a character, and such habits, that they can hereafter find their chief happiness in giving up their will to God, and in living to do good to others, instead of living merely to please themselves.

It can be pointed out to them, that they must always submit their will to the will of God, or else be continually miserable. It can be shown how, in the nursery, and in the school, and through all future days, a child must practice the giving up of his will and wishes, when they interfere with the rights and comfort of others; and how important it is, early to learn to do this, so that it will, by habit, become easy and agreeable. It can be shown how children who are indulged in all their wishes, and who are never accustomed to any self-denial, always find it hard to refrain from what injures themselves and others. It can be shown, also, how important it is for every person to form such habits of benevolence toward others that self-denial in doing good will become easy.

Parents have learned, by experience, that children can be constrained by authority and penalties to exercise self-denial, for *their own* good, till a habit is formed which makes the duty comparatively easy. For example, well trained children can be accustomed to deny themselves tempting articles of food, which are injurious, until the practice ceases to be painful and difficult. Whereas, an indulged child would be thrown into fits of anger or discontent, when its wishes were crossed by restraints of this kind.

But it has not been so readily discerned, that the same method is needful in order to form a habit of self-denial in doing good to others. It has been supposed that while children must be forced, by *authority*, to be self-denying and prudent in regard to their own happiness, it may properly be left to their own discretion, whether they will practice any self-denial in doing good to others. But the more difficult a duty is, the greater is the need of parental authority in forming a habit which will make that duty easy.

In order to secure this, some parents turn their earliest efforts to this object. They require the young child always to offer to others a part of every thing which it receives; always to comply with all reasonable requests of others for service; and often to practice little acts of self-denial, in order to secure some enjoyment for others. If one child receives a present of some nicety, he is required to share it with all his brothers and sisters. If one asks his brother to help him in some study or sport, and is met with a denial, the parent requires the unwilling child to act benevolently, and give up some of his time to increase his brother's enjoyment. Of course, in such an effort as this, discretion must be used as to the frequency and extent of the exercise of authority, to induce a habit of benevolence. But where parents deliberately aim at such an object, and wisely conduct their instructions and discipline to secure it, very much will be accomplished.

Those, again, who will join with children and help them in their sports, will learn by this mode to understand the feelings and interests of childhood; while at the same time, they secure a degree of confidence and affection which can not be gained so easily in any other way.

And it is to be regretted that parents so often relinquish this most powerful mode of influence to domestics and playmates, who often use it in the most pernicious manner. In joining in such sports, older persons should never yield entirely the attitude of superiors, or allow disrespectful manners or address. And respectful deportment is never more cheerfully accorded, than in seasons when young hearts are pleased and made grateful by having their tastes and enjoyments so efficiently promoted.

Next to the want of all government, the two most fruitful sources of evil to children are, *unsteadiness* in government and *over-government*. Most of the cases in which the children of sensible and conscientious parents turn out badly, result from one or the other of these causes. In cases of unsteady government, either one parent is very strict, severe and unbending, and the other excessively indulgent, or else the parents are sometimes very strict and decided, and at other times allow disobedience to go unpunished. In such cases, children, never knowing exactly when they can escape with impunity, are constantly tempted to make the trial.

The bad effects of this can be better appreciated by reference to one important principle of the mind. It is found to be universally true, that, when any object of desire is put entirely beyond the reach of hope or expectation, the mind very soon ceases to long for it, and turns to other objects of pursuit. But so long as the mind is hoping for some good, and making efforts to obtain it, any opposition excites irritable feelings. Let the object be put entirely beyond all hope, and this irritation soon ceases.

In consequence of this principle, those children who are under the care of persons of steady and decided government know that whenever a thing is forbidden or

denied, it is out of the reach of hope; the desire, therefore, soon ceases, and they turn to other objects. But the
children of undecided, or of over-indulgent parents, never
enjoy this preserving aid. When a thing is denied, they
never know but either coaxing may win it, or disobedience secure it without any penalty, and so they are kept
in that state of hope and anxiety which produces irritation and tempts to insubordination. The children of
very indulgent parents, and of those who are undecided
and unsteady in government, are very apt to become
fretful, irritable, and fractious.

Another important maxim is, Try to keep children in
a happy state of mind. Every one knows, by experience,
that it is easier to do right and submit to rule when cheerful and happy, than when irritated. This is peculiarly
true of children; and a wise mother, when she finds her
child fretful and impatient, and thus constantly doing
wrong, will often remedy the whole difficulty, by telling
some amusing story, or by getting the child engaged in
some amusing sport. This strongly shows the importance
of learning to govern children without the employment
of angry tones, which always produce irritation.

In forming the moral habits of children, it is wise to
take into account the peculiar temptations to which they
are to be exposed. The people of this nation are emi-
nently a trafficking people; and the present standard of
honesty, as to trade and debts, is very low, and every year
seems sinking still lower. It is, therefore, preëminently
important, that children should be trained to strict *honesty,* both in word and deed. It is not merely teaching
children to avoid absolute lying, which is needed: *all
kinds of deceit* should be guarded against; and all kinds
of little dishonest practices be strenuously opposed. A
child should be brought up with the determined princi-

ple, never to *run in debt,* but to be content to live in a humbler way, in order to secure that true independence, which should be the noblest distinction of an American citizen.

There is no more important duty devolving upon a mother, than the cultivation of habits of modesty and propriety in young children. All indecorous words or deportment should be carefully restrained; and delicacy and reserve studiously cherished. It is a common notion, that it is important to secure these virtues to one sex, more than to the other; and, by a strange inconsistency, the sex most exposed to danger is the one selected as least needing care. Yet a wise mother will be especially careful that her sons are trained to modesty and purity of mind.

Yet few mothers are sufficiently aware of the dreadful penalties which often result from indulged impurity of thought. If children, in *future* life, can be preserved from licentious associates, it is supposed that their safety is secured. But the records of our insane retreats, and the pages of medical writers, teach that even in solitude, and without being aware of the sin or the danger, children may inflict evils on themselves, which not unfrequently terminate in disease, delirium, and death.

There is no necessity for explanations on this point any farther than this; that certain parts of the body are not to be touched except for purposes of cleanliness, and that the most dreadful suffering comes from disobeying these commands. So in regard to practices and sins of which a young child will sometimes inquire, the wise parent will say, that this is what children can not understand, and about which they must not talk or ask questions. And they should be told that it is always a bad sign, when children talk on matters which parents call vulgar and indecent, and that the company of such children should be avoided. Disclosing details of wrong-doing to young and curious children, often leads to the very evils feared. But parents and teachers, in this age of danger, should be well informed and watchful; for it is not unfrequently the case, that servants and school-mates will teach young children practices, which exhaust the nervous system and bring on paralysis, mania, and death.

And finally, in regard to the early religious training of children, the examples of the Creator in the early training of our race may safely be imitated. That "He is, and is a rewarder"—that he is everywhere present—that he is a tender Father in heaven, who is grieved when any of his children do wrong, yet ever ready to forgive those who are striving to please him by well-doing, these are the most effective motives to save the young from the paths of danger and sin. The rewards and penalties of the life to come are better adapted to maturer age, than to the imperfect and often false and fearful conceptions of the childish mind.

6.   Ministry of Women*

In a series of articles written for the popular Harper's
New Monthly Magazine, *Catharine Beecher provided
blueprints for a home which would manifest proper
attitudes toward the wife and mother. Joining cooking,
eating, and living areas, stressing "family" rooms, open
spaces, the "tempting" hearth, and labor-saving arrangements, she translated her idyl of domestic life into archi-
tectural forms which could transform the habits of the
nation.*

In this Magazine for November, 1864, it was shown that
woman's *distinctive profession* includes three departments—the training of the mind in childhood, the nursing of infants and of the sick, and all the handicrafts and
management of the family state. With perhaps the excep-
tion of the school training of children, it was claimed
that the profession of woman is *socially disgraced,* so that
no woman of culture and refinement, in the wealthy
classes, would resort to cooking, chamber-work, or nursing infants and the sick for a livelihood, scarcely any
more than their brothers would resort to burglary or
piracy.

It was shown also that women are not *trained* for their

* Catharine E. Beecher, "How to Redeem Woman's Profession
from Dishonor," *Harper's New Monthly Magazine,* XXXI (1865),
710–716, abridged.

profession as men are for theirs; that there is no provision made for it in public or private schools; and that every school, as well as other social influence, tends at once to disgrace woman's profession and to destroy her health.

Woman, as well as man, was made to *work;* and her Maker has adapted her body to its appropriate labor. The tending of children and doing house-work exercise those very muscles which are most important to woman-hood; while neglecting to exercise the arms and trunk causes dangerous debility in most delicate organs.

Our early mothers worked and trained their daughters to work, and thus became healthy, energetic, and cheer-ful. But in these days, young girls, in the wealthy classes, do not use the muscles of their body and arms in domestic labor or in any other way. Instead of this, study and read-ing stimulate the brain and nerves to debility by excess, while the muscles grow weak for want of exercise. Thus the whole constitution is weakened.

In consequence of this there is a universal lamentation over the decay of the female constitution and the ruined health of both women and girls. At the same time vast numbers are without honorable compensating employ-ment, so that in the wealthy circles unmarried women suffer from aimless vacuity, and in the poorer classes from unrequited toil and consequent degradation and vice.

When houses are built *on Christian principles* women of wealth and culture will *work themselves, and train their children to work,* instead of having ignorant for-eigners to ruin their food in a filthy kitchen, and ruin their children in the nursery.

When houses are built to honor woman's profession, and to secure the beauty, order, and comfort of a per-fected house, the kitchen, as it usually exists, will be banished. Instead of the dark and comfortless room for family work, there will be one provided with sunlight and pure air, and well supplied with utensils and comforts in tasteful and convenient forms. So woman's dress will be not only neat and convenient but tasteful, as much so in the working-room as in the parlor.

Woman's work will be honorable and tasteful and agreeable when *cultivated* women undertake to make it so.

And when women of refinement and culture build houses on the Christian and democratic plan, work themselves, and train their children to work, they will never suffer for want of domestic helpers. Instead of coarse and vulgar servants, who live in the cellar and sleep in the garret, they will have refined and sympathizing friends to train their children, nurse their sick, and share in all their comforts, joys, and sorrows.

A time will come when women will give as liberally to elevate the true profession of women as *the ministers of home,* as they have to elevate the professions of men.

The remainder of this article will give drawings and descriptions to illustrate one house constructed on democratic and Christian principles. It is designed for persons in easy circumstances, who begin housekeeping with the true Christian idea of training a young family *to work* as well as to practice all the other social and domestic virtues.

Every family, as the general rule, includes the parents as the educators, and the children to be trained to Christian life. To these are added aged parents or infirm and homeless relatives. These are preserved in life after their active usefulness ceases, and often when they would gladly depart, for the special benefit of the young, as the only mode in which, in early life, they can be trained to self-sacrificing benevolence, to reverence for the aged, and to tender sympathy for the sick and unfortunate. Instead of regarding such members of a family as a burden and annoyance, the wise and Christian parents will welcome them as suffering helpers aiding to develop the highest Christian virtues in their children.

This house is planned for a family of ten or twelve, which may be regarded as the average number in healthy families.

The *site* is a dry spot with a cellar well drained, in an open space, where the health-giving sun falls on every part, and the house so placed that the rooms in common use shall have the sun all day.

A *form* nearest a square best secures sunlight, perfect ventilation, and economical arrangement. Every projection increases expense and diminishes the chances of sunlight, proper warming, and ventilation.

The *close packing of conveniences,* so as to save time and steps, and contrivances to avoid the multiplication of rooms to be furnished, cleaned, and kept in order, is indispensable to economy of time, labor, and expense. In many large kitchens, with various closets, half the time of a cook is employed in walking to collect her utensils and materials, which all might be placed together.

The *stove* is placed between the dish and cooking closet, inclosed by partitions to the wall, with rising or sliding doors. A sliding closet, D W, to raise wood and coal from the cellar. Thus the stove can be entirely open in cold weather, and in the warm season closed tight with a contrivance to carry off the hot air and the smells of cooking into a ventilating flue. In warm weather the stove is used for baking by moving the sliding-door, to be immediately closed after using the oven. These slid-

ing partitions or doors, hung like windows, are made of
wood, and lined with tin next the stove.

By this arrangement when the folding-doors of the
Family Room are open there is a large and airy room for
work-hours, and every article and utensil close at hand.

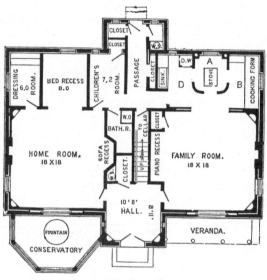

PLAN OF FIRST FLOOR.

When work is over and the folding-doors closed the room
is a cheerful sitting-room for the family. It is furnished
with a cheerful green carpet, and the appended work-
closets are covered with a light green oil-cloth to match
the carpet. On one side is a closet, for china, glass, and
silver, with a small sink for washing them. In two corners
are niches for busts and flowers, with small closets under
them for working conveniences. A fire-place and mantle

ornaments tempt the family gathering around the social hearth. The room opens to the piazza by sliding-doors. Glass roof and partitions in winter can turn this into a green-house, warmed by a register. On one side is a recess for a piano. This and the adjacent room to have *deadened* walls, so that the mother, if weary or ill, can find perfect quiet in the Home Room below or the Library above. The wearisome practicing of children on a piano will be thus escaped.

The stationary dining-table has appendages and conveniences *under* it, as do the *ottomans* with lids, which serve to store newspapers and other matters. By such arrangements many steps are saved and order promoted. The *covers* of the sofa, ottomans, and table, and the wall-paper should match in color and design with the carpet, as also the window-shades. Such arrangements as these save the labor and expense of separate kitchen and dining-room, and also the expense of wasteful domestics. In such a house parents could train their children to be their happy associates in both work and play.

The West Room is specially for parents and children, and is named the *Home Room*. On the north is a bed recess concealed by folding-doors or curtains. On one side is the parents' dressing-room, with drawers on one side to the ceiling, and a clothes-press. The other side is the children's room, with drawers and clothes-press, close to the bath and water-closet and back outside door, so that children can run out and in without using other parts of the house. On one side of the back-door is a closet for garden tools and shoes, and on the other side a wash-bowl and towel, with a towel closet at hand, near both to this and to the bath-room.

The Home Room opens to a south conservatory and small fountain. Here parents can train their children to love and rear flowers, *not for themselves* alone, but for those who are less favored. Every child can not only give flowers to friends, but save seeds to give to some poor children, and *teach them how* to adorn their own homes with such blossoms of love and beauty. A sofa recess is in this room, and two niches in the opposite corners with work-closets under, while the centre-table and ottomans are provided with hidden places for storing conveniences. The bed recess and dressing-rooms are so provided with drawers and closets, *reaching to the wall,* that every article needed by parents and children may be stored close at hand. Windows in each division, and openings over partitions, secure ventilation.

At night, the parents and two little ones have a large and airy bedroom. In the day, these doors being closed, the same room is a nursery or a parlor at pleasure.

A house on this plan will accommodate a family of ten, and afford also a guest-chamber, and it offers all the conveniences and comforts and most of the elegances of houses that cost four times the amount and require three or four servants.

If a new-married pair commence housekeeping in it, the young wife, aided by a girl of ten or twelve, could easily perform all the labor except the washing and ironing, which could be done by hired labor in the basement. The first months of housekeeping could be spent in perfecting herself and her assistant, whom she could train to do all kinds of family work, and also to be her intelligent and sympathizing helper when children come.

While it should be the aim to render woman's profession so honorable that persons of the highest position and culture will seek it, as men seek their most honored professions, there must still be the class of *servants,* to carry out a style of living and expenditure both lawful and useful, where large fortunes abound. For this class the aim should be to secure their thorough preparation and to increase their advantages. Should both aims be achieved, then a woman who prefers a style of living demanding servants, will be so trained herself as not to be dependent on hirelings at the sacrifice of self-respect. On the other hand, a woman who chooses another style of living, so as to work herself and train her children to work, can do so without fear of losing any social advantages. Or, in case more helpers are needed, she can secure highly cultivated and refined *friends* to share all her family enjoyments, instead of depending on a class inferior in cultivation and less qualified to form the habits and tastes of her children.

One aim of this article is to attract the notice of conscientious persons commencing the family state with means sufficient for a much more expensive establishment.

Many such really believe themselves the followers of Christ who have seldom practiced that economy which denies self to increase the advantages of the poor, especially in deciding on the *style of living* they adopt. Most wealthy persons provide houses, equipage, servants, and expenditures that demand most of their income, while the waste in their kitchens alone would, by careful economy, such as we see in France, feed another whole family.

When houses are built on Christian and democratic principles, and young girls in every condition of life are trained to a wise economy, thousands of young men, who can not afford to marry young ladies trained in the common boarding-school fashion, will find the chief impediment removed; and thus healthful and happy homes will multiply with our increasing wealth and culture.

II

Margaret Fuller

7. Father*

*Like Catharine Beecher, Margaret Fuller was dominated
by her father. Margaret's recollections of Timothy Fuller,
however, were always sharpened by resentment. As a
child, she had known that he thought her sister prettier
than herself, and that her own role was perforce intellectual; desperate to please, she had been scared by his
ambitions for her. Though the training Margaret's father
gave her made her a learned woman, able to discomfit a
Holmes or an Emerson, she remained convinced that this
education had been dead wrong; and calling upon theories of hygiene familiar to Catharine Beecher, she
blamed her "morbid temperament" upon her forced
precocity.*

My father,—all whose feelings were now concentrated
on me,—instructed me himself. The effect of this was so
far good that, not passing through the hands of many
ignorant and weak persons as so many do at preparatory
schools, I was put at once under discipline of consider-
able severity, and, at the same time, had a more than
ordinarily high standard presented to me. My father was
a man of business, even in literature; he had been a high
scholar at college, and was warmly attached to all he had
learned there, both from the pleasure he had derived in

* *Memoirs of Margaret Fuller Ossoli* (Boston: Phillips, Sampson,
and Co., 1852), I, 14–16.

the exercise of his faculties and the associated memories of success and good repute. He was, beside, well read in French literature, and in English, a Queen Anne's man. He hoped to make me the heir of all he knew, and of as much more as the income of his profession enabled him to give me means of acquiring. At the very beginning, he made one great mistake, more common, it is to be hoped, in the last generation, than the warnings of physiologists will permit it to be with the next. He thought to gain time, by bringing forward the intellect as early as possible. Thus I had tasks given me, as many and various as the hours would allow, and on subjects beyond my age; with the additional disadvantage of reciting to him in the evening, after he returned from his office. As he was subject to many interruptions, I was often kept up till very late; and as he was a severe teacher, both from his habits of mind and his ambition for me, my feelings were kept on the stretch till recitations were over. Thus frequently, I was sent to bed several hours too late, with nerves unnaturally stimulated. The consequence was a premature development of the brain, that made me a "youthful prodigy" by day, and by night a victim of spectral illusions, nightmare, and somnambulism, which at the time prevented the harmonious development of my bodily powers and checked my growth, while, later, they induced continual headache, weakness and nervous affections, of all kinds. As these again re-acted on the brain, giving undue force to every thought and every feeling, there was finally produced a state of being both too active and too intense, which wasted my constitution, and will bring me,—even although I have learned to understand and regulate my now morbid temperament,—to a premature grave.

No one understood this subject of health then. No one

knew why this child, already kept up so late, was still un-willing to retire. My aunts cried out upon the "spoiled child, the most unreasonable child that ever was,—if brother could but open his eyes to see it,—who was never willing to go to bed." They did not know that, so soon as the light was taken away, she seemed to see colossal faces advancing slowly towards her, the eyes dilating, and each feature swelling loathsomely as they came, till at last, when they were about to close upon her, she started up with a shriek which drove them away, but only to return when she lay down again. They did not know that, when at last she went to sleep, it was to dream of horses tramp-ling over her, and to awake once more in fright; or, as she had just read in her Virgil, of being among trees that dripped with blood, where she walked and walked and could not get out, while the blood became a pool and splashed over her feet, and rose higher and higher, till soon she dreamed it would reach her lips. No wonder the child arose and walked in her sleep, moaning all over the house, till once, when they heard her, and came and waked her, and she told what she had dreamed, her father sharply bid her "leave off thinking such nonsense, or she would be crazy,"—never knowing that he was himself the cause of all these horrors of the night. Often she dreamed of following to the grave the body of her mother, as she had done that of her sister, and woke to find the pillow drenched in tears. These dreams softened her heart too much, and cast a deep shadow over her young days; for then, and later, the life of dreams,— probably because there was in it less to distract the mind from its own earnestness,—has often seemed to her more real, and been remembered with more interest, than that of waking hours.

Poor child! Far remote in time, in thought, from that

period, I look back on these glooms and terrors, wherein I was enveloped, and perceive that I had no natural childhood.

8. Schoolteaching*

Unlike Catharine Beecher, Margaret Fuller resented having to be a schoolteacher; she would have preferred to write the life of Goethe. In 1837, however, needing money for herself and her family, she became head teacher at the Greene Street School, in Providence, Rhode Island. In the following excerpts from letters, she describes her arrival, her aims, and her departure. Though her students came to adore her, she left the school with some relief, informing Channing that she now hoped to do something for women.

The new institution of which I am to be "Lady Superior" was dedicated last Saturday. People talk to me of the good I am to do; but the last fortnight has been so occupied in the task of arranging many scholars of various ages and unequal training, that I cannot yet realize this new era.

The gulf is vast, wider than I could have conceived possible, between me and my pupils; but the sight of such deplorable ignorance, such absolute burial of the best powers, as I find in some instances, makes me comprehend, better than before, how such a man as Mr. Alcott could devote his life to renovate elementary education. I have pleasant feelings when I see that a new world has already been opened to them.

• *Memoirs of Margaret Fuller Ossoli* (Boston: Phillips, Sampson, and Co., 1852), I, 177–180.

Nothing of the vulgar feeling towards teachers, too often to be observed in schools, exists towards me. The pupils seem to reverence my tastes and opinions in all things; they are docile, decorous, and try hard to please; they are in awe of my displeasure, but delighted whenever permitted to associate with me on familiar terms. As I treat them like ladies, they are anxious to prove that they deserve to be so treated.

There is room here for a great move in the cause of education, and if I could resolve on devoting five or six years to this school, a good work might, doubtless, be done. Plans are becoming complete in my mind, ways and means continually offer, and, so far as I have tried them, they succeed. I am left almost as much at liberty as if no other person was concerned. Some sixty scholars are more or less under my care, and many of them begin to walk in the new paths pointed out. General activity of mind, accuracy in processes, constant looking for principles, and search after the good and the beautiful, are the habits I strive to develop.

I will write a short record of the last day at school. For a week past I have given the classes in philosophy, rhetoric, history, poetry, and moral science, short lectures on the true objects of study, with advice as to their future course; and to-day, after recitation, I expressed my gratification that the minds of so many had been opened to the love of good and beauty.

Then came the time for last words. First, I called into the recitation room the boys who had been under my care. They are nearly all interesting, and have showed a chivalric feeling in their treatment of me. People talk of women not being able to govern boys; but I have always found it a very easy task. He must be a coarse boy, indeed, who, when addressed in a resolute, yet gentle manner, by a lady, will not try to merit her esteem. These boys have always rivalled one another in respectful behavior. I spoke a few appropriate words to each, mentioning his peculiar errors and good deeds, mingling some advice with more love, which will, I hope, make it remembered. We took a sweet farewell. With the younger girls I had a similar interview.

Then I summoned the elder girls, who have been my especial charge. I reminded them of the ignorance in which some of them were found, and showed them how all my efforts had necessarily been directed to stimulating their minds,—leaving undone much which, under other circumstances, would have been deemed indispensable. I thanked them for the favorable opinion of my government which they had so generally expressed, but specified three instances in which I had been unjust. I thanked them, also, for the moral beauty of their conduct, bore witness that an appeal to conscience had never failed, and told them of my happiness in having the faith thus confirmed, that young persons can be best guided by addressing their highest nature. I declared my consciousness of having combined, not only in speech but in heart, tolerance and delicate regard for the convictions of their parents, with fidelity to my own, frankly uttered. I assured them of my true friendship, proved by my never having cajoled or caressed them into good. Every word of praise had been earned; all my influence over them was rooted in reality; I had never softened nor palliated their faults; I had appealed, not to their weakness, but to their strength; I had offered to them, always, the loftiest motives, and had made every other end subordinate to that of spiritual growth. With a heartfelt blessing, I dismissed them; but none stirred, and we all sat for some moments, weeping. Then I went round the circle and bade each, separately, farewell.

9. Conversations*

Margaret Fuller's plan to do something for women materialized in a new sort of education. In the first selection, a letter to Mrs. George Ripley which was "intended for circulation," she set forth her goal. The next four excerpts describe what actually took place when Margaret's friends gathered for her classes: the first two are Margaret's accounts; the last two, descriptions by participants. The final selection, one of ten conversations published by a young friend, was dubbed "dull" by the reporter. To the reader, however, the discussion of Bacchus seems much like the other conversations, uniting Margaret's "mountain ME"; the group's free-swinging references to the arts, their lives, and the gods; and the imperturbability of exalted motive.

My dear friend:—The advantages of a weekly meeting, for conversation, might be great enough to repay the trouble of attendance, if they consisted only in supplying a point of union to well-educated and thinking women, in a city which, with great pretensions to mental refinement, boasts, at present, nothing of the kind, and where I have heard many, of mature age, wish for some such means of stimulus and cheer, and those younger, for a

* *Memoirs of Margaret Fuller Ossoli* (Boston: Phillips, Sampson, and Co., 1852), I, 324–333, abridged; *Margaret and Her Friends, or, Ten Conversations with Margaret Fuller*, reported by Caroline W. Healey (Boston: Roberts Brothers, 1895), pp. 156–162.

place where they could state their doubts and difficulties, with a hope of gaining aid from the experience or aspirations of others. And, if my office were only to suggest topics, which would lead to conversation of a better order than is usual at social meetings, and to turn back the current when digressing into personalities or commonplaces, so that what is valuable in the experience of each might be brought to bear upon all, I should think the object not unworthy of the effort.

But my ambition goes much further. It is to pass in review the departments of thought and knowledge, and endeavor to place them in due relation to one another in our minds. To systematize thought, and give a precision and clearness in which our sex are so deficient, chiefly, I think, because they have so few inducements to test and classify what they receive. To ascertain what pursuits are best suited to us, in our time and state of society, and how we may make best use of our means for building up the life of thought upon the life of action.

Could a circle be assembled in earnest, desirous to answer the questions,—What were we born to do? and how shall we do it?—which so few ever propose to themselves till their best years are gone by, I should think the undertaking a noble one, and, if my resources should prove sufficient to make me its moving spring, I should be willing to give to it a large portion of those coming years, which will, as I hope, be my best. I look upon it with no blind enthusiasm, nor unlimited faith, but with a confidence that I have attained a distinct perception of means, which, if there are persons competent to direct them, can supply a great want, and promote really high objects. So far as I have tried them yet, they have met with success so much beyond my hopes, that my faith will not easily be shaken, nor my earnestness chilled. Should I, however, be disappointed in Boston, I could hardly hope that such a plan could be brought to bear on general society, in any other city of the United States. But I do not fear, if a good beginning can be made. I am confident that twenty persons cannot be brought together from better motives than vanity or pedantry, to talk upon such subjects as we propose, without finding in themselves great deficiencies, which they will be very desirous to supply.

Should the enterprise fail, it will be either from incompetence in me, or that sort of vanity in them which wears the garb of modesty. On the first of these points, I need not speak. I cannot be supposed to have felt so much the wants of others, without feeling my own still more deeply. And, from the depth of this feeling, and the earnestness it gave, such power as I have yet exerted has come. Of course, those who are inclined to meet me, feel a confidence in me, and should they be disappointed, I shall regret it not solely or most on my own account. I have not given my gauge without measuring my capacity to sustain defeat. For the other, I know it is very hard to lay aside the shelter of vague generalities, the art of coterie criticism, and the "delicate disdains" of *good society,* and fearlessly meet the light, even though it flow from the sun of truth. Yet, as, without such generous courage, nothing of value can be learned or done, I hope to see many capable of it; willing that others should think their sayings crude, shallow, or tasteless, if, by such unpleasant means, they may attain real health and vigor, which need no aid from rouge or candlelight, to brave the light of the world.

Since I saw you, I have been told of persons who are desirous to join the class, "if only they need not talk." I am so sure that the success of the whole depends on conversation being general, that I do not wish any one to come, who does not intend, if possible, to take an active part. No one will be forced, but those who do not talk will not derive the same advantages with those who openly state their impressions, and can consent to have it known that they learn by blundering, as is the destiny of man here below. And general silence, or side talks, would paralyze me. I should feel coarse and misplaced, were I to harangue over-much. In former instances, I have been able to make it easy and even pleasant, to twenty-five out of thirty, to bear their part, to question, to define, to state, and examine opinions. If I could not do as much now, I should consider myself as unsuccessful, and should withdraw. But I shall expect communication to be effected by degrees, and to do a great deal myself at the first meetings. My method has been to open a subject,— for instance, Poetry, as expressed in—

External Nature;
The life of man;
Literature;
The fine arts;

or, The history of a nation to be studied in—

Its religious and civil institutions;
Its literature and arts;
The characters of its great men;

and, after as good a general statement as I know how to make, select a branch of the subject, and lead others to give their thoughts upon it. When they have not been successful in verbal utterance of their thoughts, I have asked them to attempt it in writing. At the next meeting, I would read these "skarts of pen and ink" aloud, and canvass their adequacy, without mentioning the names of the writers. I found this less necessary, as I proceeded, and my companions attained greater command both of thought and language; but for a time it was useful, and may be now. Great advantage in point of discipline may be derived from even this limited use of the pen.

I do not wish, at present, to pledge myself to any course of subjects. Generally, I may say, they will be such as literature and the arts present in endless profusion. Should a class be brought together, I should wish, first, to ascertain our common ground, and, in the course of a few meetings, should see whether it be practicable to follow out the design in my mind, which, as yet, would look too grand on paper.

Let us see whether there will be any organ, before noting down the music to which it may give breath.

*   *   *

My class is prosperous. I was so fortunate as to rouse, at once, the tone of simple earnestness, which can scarcely, when once awakened, cease to vibrate. All seem in a glow, and quite as receptive as I wish. They question and examine, yet follow leadings; and thoughts, not opinions, have ruled the hour every time. There are about twenty-five members, and every one, I believe, full of interest. The first time, ten took part in the conversation; the last, still more. Mrs.———came out in a way that surprised me. She seems to have shaken off a wonderful number of films. She showed pure vision, sweet sincerity, and much talent. Mrs.— ——keeps us in good order, and takes care that Christianity and morality are not forgotten. The first day's topic was, the genealogy of heaven and earth; then the Will, (Jupiter); the Understanding, (Mercury): the second day's, the celestial inspiration of genius, perception and transmission of divine law, (Apollo); the terrene inspiration, the impassioned abandonment of genius, (Bacchus). Of the thunderbolt, the caduceus, the ray, and the grape, having disposed as well

as might be, we came to the wave, and the sea-shell it
moulds to Beauty, and Love her parent and her child.

I assure you, there is more Greek than Bostonian spoken at the meetings; and we may have pure honey of
Hymettus to give you yet.

*   *   *

The circle I meet interests me. So even devoutly
thoughtful seems their spirit, that, from the very first, I
took my proper place, and never had the feeling I
dreaded, of display, of a paid Corinne. I feel as I would,
truly a teacher and a guide. All are intelligent; five or
six have talent. But I am never driven home for ammuni-
tion; never put to any expense; never truly called out.
What I have is always enough; though I feel how superficially I am treating my subject.

*   *   *

"Women are now taught, at school, all that men are;
they run over, superficially, even *more* studies, without
being really taught anything. When they come to the business of life, they find themselves inferior, and all their
studies have not given them that practical good sense,
and mother wisdom, and wit, which grew up with our
grandmothers at the spinning-wheel. But, with this difference; men are called on, from a very early period, to
reproduce all that they learn. Their college exercises,
their political duties, their professional studies, the first
actions of life in any direction, call on them to put to use
what they have learned. But women learn without any
attempt to reproduce. Their only reproduction is for
purposes of display."

"It is to supply this defect," Miss Fuller said, "that
these conversations have been planned." She was not

here to teach; but she had had some experience in the management of such a conversation as was now proposed; she meant to give her view on each subject, and provoke the thoughts of others.

"It would be best to take subjects on which we know words, and have vague impressions, and compel ourselves to define those words. We should have, probably, mortifications to suffer; but we should be encouraged by the rapid gain that comes from making a simple and earnest effort for expression."

Miss Fuller had proposed the Grecian Mythology as the subject of the first conversations, and now gave her reasons for the choice. "It is quite separated from all exciting local subjects. It is serious, without being solemn, and without excluding any mode of intellectual action; it is playful, as well as deep. It is sufficiently wide, for it is a complete expression of the cultivation of a nation. It is objective and tangible. It is, also, generally known, and associated with all our ideas of the arts."

"It originated in the eye of the Greek. He lived out of doors: his climate was genial, his senses were adapted to it. He was vivacious and intellectual, and personified all he beheld. He *saw* the oreads, naiads, nereids. Their forms, as poets and painters give them, are the very lines of nature humanized, as the child's eye sees faces in the embers or in the clouds."

"Other forms of the mythology, as Jupiter, Juno, Apollo, are great instincts, or ideas, or facts of the internal constitution, separated and personified."

After exhibiting their enviable mental health, and rebutting the cavils of some of the speakers,—who could not bear, in Christian times, by Christian ladies, that heathen Greeks should be envied,—Miss Fuller declared, "that she had no desire to go back, and believed we have the elements of a deeper civilization; yet, the Christian was in its infancy; the Greek in its maturity; nor could she look on the expression of a great nation's intellect, as insignificant. These fables of the Gods were the result of the universal sentiments of religion, aspiration, intellectual action, of a people, whose political and æsthetic life had become immortal; and we must leave off despising, if we would begin to learn."

Miss Fuller's thoughts were much illustrated, and all was said with the most captivating address and grace, and with beautiful modesty. The position in which she placed herself with respect to the rest, was entirely ladylike, and companionable. She told what she intended, the earnest purpose with which she came, and, with great tact, indicated the indiscretions that might spoil the meeting.

* * *

Christmas made a holiday for Miss Fuller's class, but it met on Saturday, at noon. As I sat there, my heart overflowed with joy at the sight of the bright circle, and I longed to have you by my side, for I know not where to look for so much character, culture, and so much love of truth and beauty, in any other circle of women and girls. The names and faces would not mean so much to you as to me, who have seen more of the lives, of which they are the sign. Margaret, beautifully dressed, (don't despise that, for it made a fine picture,) presided with more dignity and grace than I had thought possible. The subject was Beauty. Each had written her definition, and Margaret began with reading her own. This called forth questions, comments, and illustrations, on all sides. The style and manner, of course, in this age, are different, but the question, the high point from which it was con-

sidered, and the earnestness and simplicity of the discussion, as well as the gifts and graces of the speakers,
gave it the charm of a Platonic dialogue. There was no
pretension or pedantry in a word that was said. The tone
of remark and question was simple as that of children in
a school class; and, I believe, every one was gratified.

*   *   *

Few present. Our last talk, and we were all dull. For my
part, Bacchus does not inspire me, and I was sad because
it was the last time that I should see Margaret. She does
not love me; I could not venture to follow her into her
own home, and I love her so much! Her life hangs on a
thread. Her face is full of the marks of pain. Young as I
am, I feel old when I look at her.

Margaret spoke of Hercules as representing the course
of the solar year. The three apples were the three seasons
of four months each into which the ancients divided it.
The twelve labors were the twelve signs.

E. P. P. accepted this, and spoke of Bryant's book,
which Margaret did not like.

Margaret said Bryant forced every fact to be a point in
a case. Bending each to his theory, he falsified it. She
wished English people would be content, like the wiser
Germans, to amass classified facts on which original
minds could act. She liked to see the Germans so content
to throw their gifts upon the pile to go down to posterity,
though the pile might carry no record of the collectors.
She spoke of Kreitzer, whose book she was now reading,
who coolly told his readers that he should not classify a
second edition afresh, for his French translator had done
it well enough, and if readers were not satisfied with his
own work, they must have recourse to the translation.
This she thought was as it ought to be.

James Clarke said it always vexed him to hear ignorant people speak of Hercules as if he were a God, and of Apollo and Jupiter as if they might at some time have been men.

Margaret said, Yes, the distinction between Gods and Demigods was that the former were the creations of pure spontaneity, and the latter actually existent personages, about whose heroic characters and lives all congenial stories clustered.

J. F. C. did not like the statues of Hercules; the brawny figure was not to his taste.

Margaret thought it majestic. She said he belonged properly to Thessaly, and was identified with its scenery. She told several little stories about him. That of his sailing round the rock of Prometheus, in a golden cup borrowed of Jupiter, was the least known. She told the story from Ovid, the glowing account of his death, of the recognition by delighted Jove. She said Wordsworth's "Tour in Greece" gave her great materials for thought.

Then she turned to Bacchus.

To show in what manner she supposed Bacchus to be the *answer* or complement to Apollo, she mentioned the statement of some late critic upon the relation of Ceres and Persephone to each other.

Persephone was the hidden energy, the vestal fire, vivifying the universe. Ceres was the productive faculty, external, bounteous. They were two phases of one thing. It was the same with Apollo and Bacchus. Apollo was the vivifying power of the sun; its genial glow stirred the earth, and its noblest product, the grape, responded.

She spoke of the Bacchanalian festivals, of the spiritual character attributed to them by Euripides, showing that originally they were something more than gross orgies.

Mrs. Clarke (Ann Wilby) said that they licensed the wildest drunkenness in Athens.

I said that was at a later time than Euripides undertook to picture. Were they identical with the Orphic? Did Orpheus really bring them from Egypt?

Margaret would accept that for a *beginning*.

E. P. P. thought that next winter we might have a talk about Roman Mythology.

Margaret liked the idea, and James Clarke seemed to accept it for the whole party. He said that he had never felt any interest in the Greek stories, until Margaret had made them the subject of conversation.

E. P. P. said she had felt excessively ashamed all through that she knew so little.

Margaret said no one need to feel so. It was a subject that might exhaust any preparation. Still, she wished we *would* study! She had herself enjoyed great advantages. Nobody's explanations had ever perplexed her brain. She had been placed in a garden, with a great pile of books before her. She began to read Latin before she read English. For a time these deities were real to her, and she prayed: "O God! if thou art Jupiter!" etc.

James Clarke said he remembered her once telling him that she prayed to Bacchus for a bunch of grapes!

Margaret smiled, and said that when she was first old enough to think about Christianity, she cried out for her dear old Greek gods. Its spirituality seemed nakedness. She could not and would not receive it. It was a long while before she saw its deeper meaning.

10. Friendship

The following letters convey the continuous moral and intellectual discipline that "friendship" involved. In her letters to Ralph Waldo Emerson, Margaret Fuller played the role of "divine mermaid or fisher of men." To women friends, she was more brusquely censorious, as her letter to the benevolent Elizabeth Peabody suggests.

RALPH WALDO EMERSON TO MARGARET FULLER*

The day is so fine that I must try to draw out of its azure magazines some ray to celebrate our friendship, and yet nature does rarely say her best words to us out of serene and splendid weather. Twilight, night, winter, & storm, the muses love, & not the halcyon hours. You must always awaken my wonder: our understanding is never perfect: so was it in this last interview, so is it ever. And yet there is progress. Ever friendly your star beams now more friendly & benign on me. I once fancied your nature & aims so eccentric that I had a foreboding that certain crises must impend in your history that would be painful to me to witness in the conviction that I could not aid even by sympathy. I said, it is so long before we can quite meet that perhaps it is better to part now, & leave

* Concord, September 25, 1840, in *The Letters of Ralph Waldo Emerson*, edited by Ralph L. Rusk (New York: Columbia University Press, 1939), II, 336–337.

our return to the Power that orders the periods of
the planets. But you have your own methods of
equipoise & recovery, without event, without convul-
sion, and I understand now your language better, I hear
my native tongue, though still I see not into you & have
not arrived at your law. Absent from you I am very likely
to deny you, and say that you lack this & that. The next
time we meet you say with emphasis that very word. I
pray you to astonish me still, & I will learn to make no
rash sentences upon you. —Now in your last letter, you,
O divine mermaid or fisher of men, to whom all gods
have given the witch-hazel-wand, or caduceus, or spirit-
discerner which detects an Immortal under every disguise
in every lurking place, (and with this you have already
unearthed & associated to yourself a whole college of
such,) do say, [for I am willing & resolute for the sake of
an instance to fix one quarrel on you,] that I am yours &
yours shall be, let me dally how long soever in this or
that other temporary relation. I on the contrary do constantly aver that you & I are not inhabitants of one
thought of the Divine Mind, but of two thoughts, that
we meet & treat like foreign states, one maritime, one in-
land, whose trade & laws are essentially unlike. I find or
fancy in your theory a certain wilfulness and not pure
acquiescence which seems to me the only authentic
mode. Our friend is part of our fate; those who dwell in
the same truth are friends; those who are exercised on
different thoughts are not, & must puzzle each other, for
the time. For the time! But who dare say how quickly the
old eternity shall swallow up the Time, or how ripe is already in either soul the augury of the dissolution of the
barriers of difference in the glimpse of ultimate unity?
—I am willing to see how unskilfully I make out a case of
difference & will open all my doors to your sunshine &

morning air. Nothing is to me more welcome nor to my recent speculation more familiar than the Protean energy by which the brute horns of Io become the cresent moon of Isis, and nature lifts itself through everlasting transition to the higher & the highest. Whoever lives must rise & grow. Life like the nimble Tartar still overleaps the Chinese wall of distinctions that had made an eternal boundary in our geography—and I who have taxed your exclusion in friendship, find you—last Wednesday, the meekest & most loving of the lovers of mankind. I thought you a great court lady with a Louis Quatorze taste for diamonds & splendor, and I find you with a "Bible in your hand," faithful to the new Ideas, beholding undaunted their tendency, & making ready your friend "to die a beggar." Honor & love to you ever from all gentle hearts—a wreath of laurel, &, far better, the wreath of olive & of palm. My little boy for whom you promised good fortune was dressed & on his feet when I came home & is recovering his good health. All things go smoothly with me in these days but myself who am much of the time but a fat weed on the lazy wharf. Lidian sends her love to you & is overjoyed to hear of "the Bible."

MARGARET FULLER TO RALPH WALDO EMERSON*

I have felt the impossibility of meeting far more than you; so much, that, if you ever know me well, you will feel that the fact of my abiding by you thus far, affords a strong proof that we are to be much to one another. How often have I left you despairing & forlorn. How often have I said, This light will never understand my fire; this

* September 29, 1840, in *The Letters of Ralph Waldo Emerson*, II, 340–341.

clear eye will never discern the law by which I am filling my circle; this simple force will never interpret my need of manifold being.

Dear friend on one point misunderstand me less. I do not love power other than every vigorous nature delights to feel itself living. To violate the sanctity of relations— I am as far from it as you can be. I make no claim. I have no wish which is not dictated by a feeling of truth. Could I lead the highest angel captive by a look, that look I would not give, unless prompted by true love: I am no usurper. I ask only mine own inheritance. If it be found that I have mistaken its boundaries, I will give up the choicest vineyard, the fairest flowergarden, to its lawful owner.

In me I did not think you saw the purity, the single-ness, into which, I have faith that all this darting motion, & restless flame shall yet be attempered & subdued. I felt that you did not for me the highest office of friendship, by offering me the clue of the labyrinth of my own being. Yet I thought you appreciated the fearlessness which shrinks from no truth in myself & others, & trusted me, believing that I knew the path for myself. O it must be that you have felt the worth of that truth which has never hesitated to infringe our relation, or aught else, rather than not vindicate itself. If you have not seen this stair on which God has been so untiringly leading me to himself, you have indeed been wholly ignorant of me. Then indeed, when my soul, in its childish agony of prayer, stretched out its arms to you as a father,—did you not see what was meant by this crying for the moon; this sullen rejection of playthings which had become un-meaning? Did you then say, "I know not what this means; perhaps this will trouble me; the time will come when I shall hide my eyes from this mood";—then you are not the friend I seek.

But did not you ask for a "foe" in your friend? Did not you ask for a "large formidable nature"? But a beautiful foe, I am not yet, to you. Shall I ever be? I know not. My life is now prayer. Through me sweetest harmonies are momently breathing. Shall they not make me beautiful, —Nay, beauty? Shall not all vehemence, all eccentricity, be purged by these streams of divine light? I have, in these hours, but one pain; The sense of the infinite exhausts & exalts: it cannot therefore possess me wholly; else, were I also one wave of gentlest force. Again I shall cease to melt & flow; again I shall seek & pierce & rend asunder.

But oh, I am now full of such sweet certainty. Never never more can it be utterly shaken. All things have I given up to the Central Power, myself, you also; yet, I cannot forbear adding, dear friend. I am now so at home, I know not how again to wander & grope, seeking my place in another soul. I need to be recognized. After this, I shall be claimed, rather than claim, yet if I speak of facts, it must be as I see them.

To L. my love. In her, I have always recognized the saintly element. *That,* better than a bible in my hand, shows that it cannot be to me wholly alien. Yet am I no saint, no anything, but a great soul born to know all, before it can return to the creative fount.

RALPH WALDO EMERSON TO MARGARET FULLER*

Today I think I shall not reply to your seven chords of

* Concord, October 1, 1840, in *The Letters of Ralph Waldo Emerson,* II, 340–341, abridged.

melody which came to me last night. I do not know how
I have ever deserved any friends. I behold them as they
approach, with wonder. If they depart from me I shall
not wonder more. And yet now & then we say things to
our mates or hear things from them which seem to put it
out of the power of the parties to be strangers again. Especially if any one show me a stroke of courage, a piece
of inventive wit, a trait of character, or a pure delight in
character when shown by others, always I must be that
man's or that woman's debtor as one who has discovered
to me among perishing men somewhat more clean & in-
corruptible than the eternal light of these midnight stars.
Indeed the only real benefit of which we are susceptible,
is, is it not?—to have man dignified for us. But I should
not write these things. I know your merriment at prov-
erbs, and only scribble that I may not send a blank sheet.
I have some pretty poetry to show you, by a young lady
who never, &c. & must try to find admittance into that
sacred grove of Jamaica before the saffron light of October shall have faded from its leaves.

But if Mr Ripley will bring you to Concord let that
be first—Fix a day,—& the earliest, I beseech you.—
though I doubt if in his *expressive* presence I shall have
one syllable of good talk with yourself. Farewell, benign
friend.

MARGARET FULLER TO
ELIZABETH PALMER PEABODY*

I wished to earlier answer your good letter, but my life
begins to be crowded and, à l'ordinaire,—pain in the

* New York, December 26, 1844, in *The Writings of Margaret Fuller*, selected and edited by Mason Wade (New York: Copyright 1941 by The Viking Press, Inc.), pp. 571–572. Reprinted by permission of The Viking Press, Inc.

side or spine follows much exertion. I am obliged to be especially careful not to write too much.

I like my position very well; think I can fill it, and learn a great deal in it. This scene brings me many fresh impressions.

Let me answer, in brief, to the most interesting part of your letter. Probably, I have, as you say, a large share of prudence by nature. It has not, however, been large enough to save me from being much disappointed, in various relations, by a want of delicacy and tenderness from those who had seemed capable of it. But, perceiving similar faults in me, and yet knowing my heart capable of pure and intelligent love, I believe them so, too, and that we shall all be better, and do better as we grow.

The tone of your letter was so mild, and its spirit so comprehensive, that I felt as if you *must* be nearer peace than I had ever expected to find you in this world. Yet your tendency to extremes, as to personal attachments, is so strong, I am afraid you will not wholly rise above it.

The persons whom you have idolized can never, in the end, be ungrateful, and, probably, at the time of retreat they still do justice to your heart. But, so long as you must draw persons too near you, a temporary recoil is sure to follow. It is the character striving to defend itself from a heating and suffocating action upon it.—

A little, only a little less of this in you would give your powers the degree of fresh air they need. Could you be as generous and sympathetic, yet never infatuated; then the blur, the haste, the tangle would disappear, and neither I nor any one could refuse to understand you.

I admit that I have never done you justice. There is so much in you that is hostile to my wishes, as to character, and especially as to the character of woman; how could I be quite candid! Yet when I have looked at you, truly, I have also looked steadily, and always feel myself in your debt that you cordially pardon all that must be to you repressing—and unpleasant in me.

To the care of the fair spirit that sometimes looks out so full through your features and your conduct I commend you. It must finally give you back all your friends.

11. Maternity

In the letters from Italy, written after the birth of her son Angelino, Margaret Fuller Ossoli described a new kind of education, in which friendship had no part. She had not become an instructed mother, in Catharine Beecher's sense; she watched her child with joyful passivity, trusting to "God and Nature" to remedy any educational lapses. Nor did she embrace a domestic ideal. She counted on total freedom for herself and her husband, fearing only that the child might have bound them to the "corrupt social contract." Yet in her journal she noted a more pressing need than liberty: "My heart was too suffocated without a child of my own. I say again I am not as strong as we thought."

MARGARET FULLER TO
ELLEN CHANNING*

The great novelty, the immense gain to me is my relation with my child. I thought the mother's heart lived in me before, but it did not. I knew nothing about it. Yet before his birth I dreaded it. I thought I should not survive, but if I did and my child did, was I not cruel to bring another into this terrible world [?] I could not at that time get any other view. When he was born that deep melancholy

* Florence, December 11, 1849, in *Margaret Fuller: American Romantic,* edited by Perry Miller (Garden City, N.Y.: Doubleday and Co., 1963), pp. 303–306, abridged.

changed once into rapture, but did not last long. Then came the prudential motherhood, then came Mrs. Edgworth, Mrs. Smith. I became a coward, a caretaker not only for the morrow but impiously faithless for twenty or thirty years ahead. I seemed wicked to have brought the little tender thing into the midst of cares and perplexities we had not feared in the least for ourselves. I imagined everything; he was to be in danger of every enormity the Croats were then committing upon the babies of Lombardy. The house would be burned over his head, but if he escaped, how were we to get money to buy his bibs and primers[?] Then his father was to be killed in the fighting, and I to die of my cough.

During the siege of Rome, I could not see my little boy. What I endured at that time, in various ways not many would survive. In the burning sun, I went every day, to wait, in the crowd, for letters about him. Often they did not come. I saw blood that streamed on the wall where Ossoli was. I have a piece of a bomb that burst close to him. I sought solace in tending the suffering men; but when I beheld the beautiful fair young men bleeding to death, or mutilated for life, I felt the woe of all the mothers who had nursed each to that full flower, to see them thus cut down. I felt the *consolation,* too,—for those youths died worthily. I was a Mater Dolorosa, and I remembered that the midwife who helped Angelino into the world came from the sign of the Mater Dolorosa. I thought, even if he lives, if he comes into the world at this great troubled time, terrible with perplexed duties, it may be to die thus at twenty years, one of a glorious hecatomb, indeed, but still a sacrifice. It seemed then I was willing he should die. But when I really saw him lingering as he did all July and August between life and death, I could not let him go unless I could go with him.

MARGARET FULLER TO
CAROLINE STURGIS TAPPAN*

I do not know what to write about him: he changes so much, has so many characters. He is like me in that, his father's character is simple and uniform, though not monotonous, more than are the flowers of spring, flowers of the valley. He is now in the most perfect rosy health, a very gay, impetuous, ardent, but sweet tempered child. He seems to me to have nothing in common with his first baby[hood (?)] with its ecstatic smiles, its exquisite sensitiveness, and a distinction in gesture and attitudes that struck everybody. His temperament seems changed by taking the milk of these robust women. His form is robust.

He is now come to quite a knowing age (fifteen months). In the morning, as soon as dressed, he signs to come into our room; then draws our curtain, kisses me rather violently, pats my face, stretches himself and says *bravo*. Then expects as a reward to be tied in his chair and have his playthings. These engage him busily, but still he calls to us to sing and drum to enliven the scene. Sometimes he calls me to kiss his hand; he laughs very much at this. Enchanting is that baby laugh, all dimples and glitter, so strangely arch and innocent. Then I wash and dress him; that is his great time. He makes it [last] as long as he can, insisting to dress and wash me the while, kicking, throwing water about, full of all manner of tricks that I think girls never dream of. Then is his walk; we have beautiful walks here for him, along the Arno, by the bridges or the sunny walk at the Cascine, protected by fine trees, always warm in mid-winter, the bands

* Florence, December 30, 1849, in *Margaret Fuller: American Romantic*, pp. 307–310, abridged.

playing in the distance and children of all ages walking
and sitting with their nurses. His walk and sleep give me
about three hours in the middle of the day. Then at eight
he goes to bed and we have the [evening]. Otherwise I
am always engaged with him. Indeed I often walk with
him, as Italian servants are not to be trusted and I feel
now [the] need of seeing him at each moment.

I feel so refreshed by his young life. Ossoli diffuses such
a power and sweetness over every day that I cannot en-
dure to think yet of our future. Too much have we suffered already trying to command it. I do not feel force to
make any effort yet. I suppose that very soon now I must
do something. I hope I shall feel able when the time
comes. I do not yet. My constitution seems making an
effort to rally, by dint of much sleep. I had slept so little
for a year and a half during the last months of preg-
nancy[,] never an hour in peace after the baby's birth,
such anxiety and anguish, when separated from him, I
was consumed as by nightly fever. I constantly started up
seeming to hear him call me. The last two months at
Rome would have destroyed almost any woman. Then,
when I went to him, he was so ill and I was constantly up
with him at night, carrying him about, feeding him. At
Perugia he began to get better. Then in [September
(manuscript is torn here, but this is the month of their
arrival)] we arrived here. The Police [threatened (?)]
to send us away. It was three weeks before we could [get]
permission to stay. Now for two months we have been
tranquil; we have resolved to repose and enjoy being together as much as we can, in this brief interval, perhaps
all we shall ever know of peace. It is very sad we have no
money, we could be so quietly happy a while. I rejoice in
all Ossoli did but the results, in this our earthly state are
disastrous, especially as my strength is now so much im-

paired. This much I do hope, in life or death, to be no more separated from Angelino.

Last winter I made the most vehement efforts at least to redeem the time, hoping thus good for the future. But, of at least two volumes written at that time, no line seems of any worth. I had suffered much constraint, much that was uncongenial, harassing, even agonizing, but this kind of pain found me unprepared. The position of a mother separated from her only child is too frightfully unnatural.

MARGARET FULLER TO
RICHARD F. FULLER*

I feel also the great responsibility about a child, and the mixture of solemn feeling with the joy its sweet ways and caresses give. Yet this is only different in degree, not in kind, from what we should feel in other relations. The destiny of all we come in contact with we may more or less impede or brighten. Much as the child lies in our power, still God and Nature are there, furnishing a thousand masters to correct our erroneous, fill up our imperfect, teachings. I feel impelled to try for good, for the sake of my child, most powerfully, but if I fail, I trust help will be tendered to him from some other quarter. I do not wish to trouble myself more than is inevitable or lose the simple, innocent pleasure of watching his growth from day to day by thinking of his future. At present my care of him is to keep him clean body and mind, to give for body and mind simple nutriment when he demands it, and to play with him. Now he learns [by] playing as

* Florence, January 8, 1850, in *Margaret Fuller: American Romantic*, pp. 310–312, abridged.

we all shall when we enter a higher state. With him my intercourse thus far has been satisfactory and if I do not well for *him* he at least has taught *me* a great deal.

Ossoli sends his love to you. I may say of him, as you say of your wife, it would be difficult to [do] other than like him, so sweet is his disposition, so without an effort disinterested, so simply wise his daily conduct, so harmonious his whole nature. Add he is a perfectly unconscious character, and never dreams that he does well. He is studying English but makes little progress. For a good while you may not be able to talk with him, but you will like showing him some of your favorite haunts: he is so happy in nature, in sweet tranquil places.

III

M. Carey Thomas

12. The "Bryn Mawr Woman"*

The following selection is an early talk that helped make M. Carey Thomas and Bryn Mawr famous. The scolding she gave Harvard's President Eliot made headlines from New York to Texas. The rambling discourse is held together by the fierce commitment to the "Bryn Mawr woman," for whom President Thomas assumed many parental responsibilities. Her elliptical notations in the manuscript include tips on etiquette ("toothpicks, knives in fish, salad"), injunctions to acquire the manner of "all people of assured position," and a continuous chant of praise for the unique clan of Bryn Mawr.

It is always my custom to welcome the students at the beginning of each academic year. I regretted very much that I was compelled to be absent on the first day, the opening of the fifteenth year of the college, but I was, I think, well employed in assisting to welcome the new President of Wellesley College. Indeed the speechmaking at Wellesley was so interesting in many ways that I shall refer to it again in a few moments and shall make some of the views on women's education there put forth the text of what I wish to speak to you about after I have given out the necessary announcements.

In our little community of students we have all grades

* M. Carey Thomas, Notes for the opening address at Bryn Mawr College, 1899 (Bryn Mawr College Archives), abridged.

represented, from Freshmen (I might almost say from even sub-Freshmen, so many scores are living at our gates) to the Faculty. This year for the first time we can begin to test the experiment of older and younger students, graduates and seniors and juniors and freshmen living together in each of our halls of residence in nearly equal proportions, instead of being massed in halls by classes. Hall association rather than class association, or rather hall association combined with class association, will, I believe, give us a far wider college culture. After all to know well sixty-five fellow students of different ages is itself to know the college world. Angles should rub off, awkwardness should disappear, the younger classmen should learn the scholarly point of view of older students, and insensibly be affected by their atmosphere, while older students learn how to influence younger students and especially graduate students, how to keep in touch with them; and so in this mutual association will, we hope, be fashioned and perfected the type of Bryn Mawr women which will, we hope, become as well known and universally admired a type as the Oxford and Cambridge man or as the graduate of the great English public schools. No such type can possibly be created except by a residence college and unless carefully divided like Oxford and Cambridge into resident halls a very large college loses the power to mould its students in external ways.

For both men and women success of every kind in after life depends greatly on gentle breeding. Doctors, lawyers, teachers, philanthropists, social leaders, everything in life in which men and women are associated together is aided or retarded by good breeding. Such breeding can best be learned at home, but in a large community like this there will always be those whose student homes are better schools of manners than the homes of other students, and living together as we do the highest standards should prevail. We all have an opportunity to correct provincialisms, uncouth pronunciations, to get rid of expressions that no person of culture could possibly use. I sometimes wonder if you know how people regard the Bryn Mawr standards and how [much] lies in your hands by some rough hoyden horse play or brutal practical joking. Manners do, as President Eliot says, matter immensely and if the Bryn Mawr woman could add to scholarship and character gentle breeding and could join high standards of behavior and usages of culture and gentle observances to high standards of scholarship we should have the type we are seeking to create.

President Carter of Williams in answering to the toast "the ideal New England college," said that he wondered sometimes if the ideal women's college in flooding with the light of learning the women within its walls could also look after the sweetness, whether sweet sixteen at entering would be sweet sixteen at graduation. Emphatically no. Sweet sixteen has the charm of childhood and ignorance that will shortly be relegated to the harems of the east.

President Eliot also said—you see that there were many doctrinaire utterances about women, for when do men gathered together on the platform of a women's college resist the attempt to shove, usually out of its path, the resistless force they see before them, which we call the higher education of women—President Eliot said that the president and faculty of a women's college had no guide from the past, that the great tradition of learning existing from the time of the Egyptians to the present existed only for men and that this vast body of inherited tradition was of no service in women's education, that women's colleges simply imitated men when they used the same educational methods instead of inventing new ones of their own and that furthermore it would indeed be strange if women's intellects were not at least as unlike men's as their bodies.

[Such a statement] only shows us that as progressive as one may be in education or other things there may be in our minds some dark spot of mediaevalism, and clearly in President Eliot's otherwise luminous intelligence women's education is this dark spot. He might as well have told the president of Wellesley to invent a new Christian religion for Wellesley or new symphonies and operas, a new Beethoven and Wagner, new statues and pictures, a new Phidias and a new Titian, new tennis, new golf, a new way to swim, skate and run, new food, and new drink. It would be easier to do all this than to create for women a new science of geography, a new Greek Tragedies, new Chemistry, new philosophies, in short, a new intellectual heavens and earth. President Taylor of Vassar in talking over this remark afterward said to me—and I think he would not object to my quoting it to you, as he told me he had often said it, that during all the years he had been educating women he had been trying to find some difference between their intellects and men's and that whenever he thought he could put his finger on a difference he found that the accuracy of his observation was overturned by future classes of students. He thought he had found but one difference, a difference of habit of life, the difference implied by women's willingness to work more hours over a difficult problem or a difficult passage of translation, whereas a man would see that a change of occupation was the proper thing and would return to attack the difficult subject after several hours of relaxation and fresh air, a woman would pore over it until she had lost her power of thinking freshly. This he accounted for by the different conditions of women's life and the fact that a woman's work in the household is never finished. I think that I may add one more difference to that suggested by President Taylor; it is this: as yet college women are not as ready to accept criticism, they are not used to the take and give of life. They have been more sheltered, less criticised and more praised.

When I was in Aix-les-Bains this summer taking the cure for sciatica, my books gave out and as I could not do serious reading during a great deal of the time I had to supply myself with the only available literature, modern French novels. In reading these novels I was very much struck with the different type of women the Anglo-Saxon race has evolved by the wider opportunities given to women of the Anglo-Saxon race. Much of the interest and tragedy of these novels turned on the doubt and distrust felt by the French husband of his wife, of his fear that she was deceiving him and that her love for him had stopped. Instead of asking her a frank question and receiving a frank reply the whole miserable drama of suspicion and jealousy and watching and spying unfolded itself. He did not ask her a question because he knew that she would deceive him. Thus, however unworthy of love and confidence women are men will love them and it is correspondingly true of women's love for men. The world is made so and the happiness of the home depends upon love and confidence between men and women. I thought as I read these novels how impossible it would be for such relations to exist between the collegebred woman and her husband. I should like to read to you a poem written by a great writer of English prose as embodying this new type of woman which we are, I hope, moulding and fashioning at Bryn Mawr College. I will close by reading Stevenson's verses: "To my Wife":

> Trusty, dusky, vivid, true,
> With eyes of gold and bramble-dew,
> Steel-true and blade-straight,
> The great artificer
> Made my mate.
>
> Honour, anger, valour, fire;
> A love that life could never tire,
>   Death quench or evil stir,
> The mighty master
>   Gave to her.

13. Education for Women and for Men*

Like many other late nineteenth-century thinkers, M. Carey Thomas saw life as a Darwinian struggle, and she was eager to get women into the fray on equal terms with men. Thus, she opposed protective legislation for female workers and, with thumping contempt and varying logic, disposed of peculiarly feminine courses, whether in piano, cooking, physiology, or parenthood.

A subject like this fairly bristles with possibilities of misunderstanding. To get a firm grip of it we must resolutely turn our minds from all side issues and endeavor to put the question in so precise a form as to make sure that we at least mean the same thing. Stripped of its non-essentials we shall find that the real question at issue has very seldom been seriously argued. Not, of course, because of its unimportance—it is all-important—but because its approaches are set round about with our dearest prejudices, especially if we are men. Logical pitfalls lie on all sides of us; controversies past and present darken the air; our path leads us thru hard-won battlefields. If we are women, our almost irresistible impulse is to slay again the slain; if we are men, the graves of our dead comrades provoke an equally irresistible desire to send a scattering

* M. Carey Thomas, "Should the Higher Education of Women Differ from That of Men?" *Educational Review*, XXI (1901), 1–10, abridged.

volley into some weak side-encampment of the enemy instead of lining up squarely for the last logical trial of arms. I have contrasted men and women advisedly, because this is one of the very few questions on which most educated men and women are to be found in opposite sides of the camp. If it were possible to discuss it dispassionately, I believe men and women could reach substantial agreement.

I will try, first of all, to state the subject of discussion so that there may be no possibility of our misunderstanding each other in regard to it; next, I will make an attempt to clear the way of prejudices and prejudgments that have really nothing at all to do with the argument; and finally, I will address myself to the argument itself. Higher education means generally any education above the high-school grade; that is, the education given in the technical and professional school as well as in the college.

In regard to technical and professional education there should, it seems to me, be little, if any, serious difference of opinion, and I shall therefore begin with that. We may differ as to whether it is desirable for a college course to precede, and be presupposed in, the course of a technical or professional school, but we cannot think that men students of law or medicine or architecture, for example, should be college-bred, while women students of law, medicine, or architecture should not. Personally I am confident that in ten years' time after graduation, physicians, and lawyers, and architects, whether men or women, whose parents have been able to send them to college, will be found to have outstripped their non-college-bred competitors both in reputation and in income. But, however we decide this matter, it must be decided in the same way for men and women.

Sex cannot affect the question of the best preliminary preparation for professional and technical study.

So also with professional and technical courses themselves. Once granted that women are to compete with men for self-support as physicians or lawyers, whether wisely or unwisely does not now concern us, being merely one of the many side issues that have in the past so obscured our judgment of the main argument; indeed, if women are not to compete there will be, of course, no women in medical schools and law schools and no reason for argument at all—the question is simply, what is the best attainable training for the physician or the lawyer, man or woman? There is no reason to believe that typhoid or scarlet fever or phthisis can be successfully treated by a woman physician in one way and by a man physician in another way. There is indeed every reason to believe that unless treated in the best way the patient may die, the sex of the doctor affecting the result less even than the sex of the patient. The question needs only to be put for us to feel irrevocably sure that there is no special woman's way of dealing with disease. And so in law, in architecture, in electricity, in bridge-building, in all mechanic arts and technical sciences, our effort must be for the most scientific instruction, the broadest basis of training that will enable men and women students to attain the highest possible proficiency in their chosen profession. Given two bridge-builders, a man and a woman, given a certain bridge to be built, and given as always the unchangeable laws of mechanics in accordance with which this special bridge and all other bridges must be built, it is simply inconceivable that the preliminary instruction given to the two bridge-builders should differ in quantity, quality, or method of presentation because while the bridge is building one will wear knickerbockers and the other a rainy-day skirt. You may say you do not think that God intended a woman to be a bridge-builder. You have, of course, a right to this prejudice; but as you live in America, and not in the interior of Asia or Africa, you will probably not be able to impose it on women who wish to build bridges. You may say that women's minds are such that they cannot build good bridges. If you are right in this opinion you need concern yourselves no further—bridges built by women will, on the whole, tend to fall down, and the competition of men who can build good bridges will force women out of the profession. Both of these opinions of yours are side issues, and, however they may be decided hereafter, do not in the remotest degree affect the main question of a common curriculum for men and women in technical and professional schools. But you may say that men and women should study bridge-building and medicine and law in separate schools, and not together. You may be foolish enough, and wasteful enough, to think that all the expensive equipment of our technical and professional schools should be duplicated for women, when experience and practice have failed to bring forward a single valid objection to professional coeducation, and when the present trend of public opinion is overwhelmingly against you; and for the sake of argument let us grant that beside every such school for men is to be founded a similar school for women. But this duplication of professional schools for women leaves us just where we were in regard to the curriculum of professional study to be taught in such women's schools. So long as men and women are to compete together, and associate together, in their professional life, women's preparation for the same profession cannot safely differ from men's. If men's preparation is better, women, who are less well prepared, will be left behind in the race; if women's is better, men will suffer in competition with women. What is best in medical training for men will be best in medical training for women; what has bad results in medical training for men will be found to have the same bad results in women's medical training. Whatever we may think of women's right to gain a livelihood in any given occupation, we must all agree that, if they are to compete successfully with men engaged in this same occupation, they must receive as thoro and prolonged a preparation for it as men. Even if we hold that women's minds differ from men's, this too is a side issue, for we must all recognize that for the purposes of successful competition it is desirable to minimize this difference by giving the *same* and not a different preparation. The greater the natural mental difference between the sexes the greater the need of a men's curriculum for professional women, if they are to hold their own in professional life after leaving the university.

The above argument applies with equal force to the training given by the university graduate school of arts and sciences. Statistics indicate that an overwhelmingly large majority of men and women graduate students are fitting themselves for the profession of higher teaching, that over one-third of all graduate students in the United States are women, and that the annual increase of women graduate students is greater than that of men. In the lower grades of teaching men have almost ceased to compete with women; in the higher grade, that is, in college teaching, women are just beginning to compete with men, and this competition is beset with the bitterest professional jealousy that women have ever had to meet, except perhaps in medicine. There are in the United States only eleven independent colleges for women of at all the same grade as the three hundred and thirty-six coeducational colleges where women and men are taught together, yet only in these separate colleges for women have women an opportunity of competing with men for professors' chairs. It is very rare indeed for coeducational colleges to employ any women instructors, and even then only so many women are as a rule employed as are needed to look after the discipline or home life of the women students. Where women are teaching in coeducational colleges side by side with men their success is regarded by men teachers with profound dislike, and on account of this sex jealousy college presidents and boards of trustees (all of whom are, as a rule, men) cannot, even if they would, materially add to the number of women teachers or advance them. The working of the elective system, however, permits us to see that men students show no such jealousy, but recognize the able teaching of women by overcrowding their classes. Women have succeeded so brilliantly, on the whole so much better than men, as primary and secondary teachers, that they will undoubtedly repeat this success in their college teaching so soon as artificial restrictions are removed. No one could seriously maintain that, handicapped as women now are by prejudice in the highest branches of a profession peculiarly their own, they should be further hampered by a professional training different from men's. Indeed, one-half of the pupils to be taught by them in schools and in colleges, if they succeed in gaining admission on an equal footing into college faculties, are boys or men who should, according to this theory, receive a training different from that of their teachers. And, further, unless we could prove that in future all women students will be taught in separate women's colleges in a different way from men students and only by differently trained women professors, we should deprive women professors who were trained differently from men in the graduate school of the power to compete successfully with men, even for chairs in women's colleges. As in medicine, law, and bridge-building, so in arts and sciences the professional work of the graduate school must from the very nature of the case be the same for men and women. Science and literature and philology are what they are and inalterable, and the objects of competition are one and the same for both men and women—instructorships and professors' chairs, scholarly fame, and power to advance, however little, the outposts of knowledge.

We have, I think, then reached substantial agreement as to the subdivision of higher education that concerns itself with professional and technical training. We are prepared to admit that when women are to compete with men in the practice of the same trade or profession, there should be as little difference as possible in their preliminary education. Further than this, I think most of us will agree that coeducation in professional and technical schools is the only economical and feasible method of educating women.

But this line of reasoning will be incomplete unless we ask ourselves whether there are not some subjects peculiar to women in which we must maintain special women's technical schools. There are certainly three professional schools where women students already largely outnumber men: normal schools, including normal departments of universities, schools of nursing, and schools for library study. If cooking and domestic service ever become lucrative professions, and more especially if men of wealth ever come to choose their wives for culinary and sanitary lore instead as at present for social and intellectual charm, such schools will tend to spring up and, like normal schools, will undoubtedly be attended almost exclusively by women. They will beyond question be taught exactly in the same way as if they were to be attended exclusively by men. The method of teaching cooking is one and the same and does not depend on the sex of the cooks. In this sense even the higher education of women in cooking will not differ from that of men. There are, however, not enough elements of intellectual growth in cooking or housekeeping to furnish a very serious or profound course of training for really intelligent women. Likewise I do not think highly of the acumen of those people who predict the coming of schools of professional training for wifehood or motherhood. What requires the harmonious balance of all our human faculties can scarcely be taught in a professional school, nor is the intellectual side sufficiently prominent to be made the subject of prolonged training.

The burden of proof is with those who believe that the college education of men and women should differ. For thirty years it has been as nearly as possible the same, with brilliantly satisfactory results, so far as concerns women. College women have married as generally as their non-college-bred sisters, and have as a rule married better than their sisters, because they have chosen a larger proportion of professional men; they have not died in childbirth, as was predicted; they have borne their proper proportion of children, and have brought up more than the usual proportion of those born; they have made efficient housekeepers and wives as well as mothers; their success as teachers has been so astonishingly great that already they are driving non-college-bred women teachers out of the field. There is, in short, not a word to be said against the success and efficiency and healthfulness of these women educated by men's curriculum.

Indeed, except practice on the piano and violin and banjo and other musical instruments, which we might have believed that women would wish in a college course, (altho most happily they do not), let us ask ourselves what other subjects peculiar to women could be introduced in a college curriculum? I have never heard more than three suggested: infant psychology, to which there is no special objection as an elective in a college curriculum (I believe, however, that as many men as women will be foolish enough—I am expressing my own point of view—to elect it, and, after all, as many college men will become fathers as college women will become mothers); chemistry with special reference to cooking, and food values and domestic science generally, which is already introduced in some coeducational colleges and will never, in my opinion, be largely elected because it lacks the wider outlook of the more general sciences and belongs rather in the technical school; and physiology with special reference to motherhood and wifehood, which is never likely to be elected voluntarily by women college students who do not know whether they will marry; nor is it, in my opinion, desirable that it should be elected. It would certainly lead to much unhappiness in married life if such courses were elected by women and not by the men they marry also. These subjects, even if we grant (which I do not) that they are especially desirable for women to study in college, would not constitute a woman's curriculum. They would simply form three electives out of many to be introduced as occasion serves into such colleges as are open to women.

Undoubtedly the life of most women after leaving

college will differ from that of men. About one-half will marry in a rather deliberate fashion, choosing carefully, and on the whole living very happily a life of comparative leisure, not of self-support; about one-third will become professional teachers, probably for life; and the greater part of the remainder will lead useful and helpful lives as unmarried women of leisure. And just because after leaving college only one-third, and that in the peculiarly limited profession of teaching, are to get the wider training of affairs that educates men engaged in business and in the professions all their lives thru, women while in college ought to have the broadest possible education. This college education should be the same as men's, not only because there is, I believe, but one best education, but because men and women are to live and work together as comrades and dear friends and married friends and lovers, and because their effectiveness and happiness and the welfare of the generation to come after them will be vastly increased if their college education has given them the same intellectual training and the same scholarly and moral ideals.

14.   The Purpose of the College*

In her frequent talks to the Bryn Mawr undergraduates, President Thomas issued a romantic and cadenced summons to live up to the college ideal. In 1907, she addressed herself to the tougher, more practical generation of the early twentieth century, welcoming its ambitions and reminding it of its Bryn Mawr heritage.

I have spoken of the students' building. The need of such a building in a college like Bryn Mawr, to be the meeting place for the various students' clubs and the centre of all the activities of student life, seems to me significant of a great change that has come over the college students in the United States. The students in our colleges are organising themselves for the study of philanthropic and social problems and for work of all kinds. Every hour of the day is apportioned between the study required by the college and organised social study through clubs of every kind, and these clubs invite by preference speakers on reform and social problems.

This means that the students in our colleges are severely practical and unsentimental in their attitude toward life. There are no longer those stretches of unoccupied leisure, those long unfilled afternoons and evenings and nights which students in my college days

* M. Carey Thomas, Notes for commencement address at Bryn Mawr College, June 6, 1907 (Bryn Mawr College Archives), abridged.

used to prize and devote to voracious and limitless reading of poetry and unending discussions of abstract questions among themselves. Wordsworth and Shelley and Keats and Browning and Swinburne and Victor Hugo were the poets of our college days; George Eliot and Balzac our novelists, and Matthew Arnold, Emerson, Carlyle, Ruskin, and Herbert Spencer our seers and prophets. Now these great teachers are read only by compulsion in English literature classes. The poet of college students, both men and women, today is Kipling, the novelists are Meredith and Tolstoi and the other Russian and Polish novelists of great social movement and vivid action; and their heroes and prophets, in so far as they have any, are the great socialistic writers and the active reform workers in our city slums and factories.

The students of today are interested in what they believe to be very modern and practical studies, apparently without regard to the relative teaching ability of the professors. Students often say to me that they wish to study these subjects because, as they say, they will help them to deal with life, and it is dealing with life that they are eager for.

The emotions which sway the young men and women students in our college mirror as in a crystal ball the coming changes in thought and action in the outside world. Young Siegfried sees dimly as in a vision the impending fight with the dragon and the fire-girt rock on which Brünhild lies asleep, and forges his sword to be in readiness.

There is, I think, very little doubt that we are entering on an age of social reconstruction and human betterment. The scientific discoveries of the last half of the past century have taught us our human race can be scientifically improved, and that we need not sit down contentedly under this stupendous weight of crime and misery and unwholesome conditions. The generation now in college is marching to the rescue. It has no time to listen to the charmed voices of classical literature and poetry.

Graduates of today—you who are to receive our degree of Master of Arts, who are in a sense doubly graduates of Bryn Mawr because you already hold our Bachelor's degree—and you who are to receive our Bachelor of Arts: we have given those of you who are commencing Bachelors today what we believe to be the best intellectual and moral discipline in the midst of what we like to think is the happiest setting of academic beauty. In the exercise of our best wisdom we have insisted on a foundation of classics, philosophy, English and science.

You are the children of your generation, the generation on whom will rest the heavy civic responsibilities which our generation turned aside. We confidently believe that your Bryn Mawr education will have fitted you to meet them. The hope of social reform lies with the young men and women leaving college to enter into active life. As I have tried to show in my address, a thousand voices are calling you to this great work— We bid you God's speed.

15.   Motives and Future
of the Educated Woman*

President Thomas spoke with confident force, partly because she saw herself as the archetypal woman of the age, moved by the Weltgeist *that made young women all over the country avid for a college education in the late 1870's. As she felt herself aligned with history, her war seemed to tap the "sex solidarity which is inevitably destined to become a compelling force in the new world." In the early twentieth century, her first battle won, she considered the prospects of the female scholars she had helped create; she called them to lives of lonely and productive dedication and asked society to give talented women a sporting chance.*

The passionate desire of women of my generation for higher education was accompanied thruout its course by the awful doubt, felt by women themselves as well as by men, as to whether women as a sex were physically and mentally fit for it. I think I can best make this clear to you if I refer briefly to my own experience. I cannot remember the time when I was not sure that studying and going to college were the things above all others which I wished to do. I was always wondering whether

* M. Carey Thomas, "Present Tendencies in Women's College and University Education," *Educational Review*, XXV (1908), 64–85, abridged.

it could be really true, as every one thought, that boys were cleverer than girls. Indeed, I cared so much that I never dared to ask any grown-up person the direct question, not even my father or mother, because I feared to hear the reply. I remember often praying about it, and begging God that if it were true that because I was a girl I could not successfully master Greek and go to college and understand things to kill me at once, as I could not bear to live in such an unjust world. When I was a little older I read the Bible entirely thru with passionate eagerness because I had heard it said that it proved that women were inferior to men. Those were not the days of the higher criticism. I can remember weeping over the account of Adam and Eve because it seemed to me that the curse pronounced on Eve might imperil girls' going to college; and to this day I can never read many parts of the Pauline epistles without feeling again the sinking of the heart with which I used to hurry over the verses referring to women's keeping silence in the churches and asking their husbands at home. I searched not only the Bible, but all other books I could get for light on the woman question. I read Milton with rage and indignation. Even as a child I knew him for the woman hater he was. The splendor of Shakspere was obscured to me then by the lack of intellectual power in his greatest women characters. Even now it seems to me that only Isabella in *Measure for measure* thinks greatly, and weighs her actions greatly, like a Hamlet or a Brutus.

I can well remember one endless scorching summer's day when sitting in a hammock under the trees with a French dictionary, blinded by tears more burning than the July sun, I translated the most indecent book I have ever read, Michelet's famous—were it not now forgotten, I should be able to say infamous—book on woman, *La femme.* I was beside myself with terror lest it might prove true that I myself was so vile and pathological a thing. Between that summer's day in 1874 and a certain day in the autumn in 1904, thirty years had elapsed. Altho during these thirty years I had read in every language every book on women that I could obtain, I had never chanced again upon a book that seemed to me so to degrade me in my womanhood as the seventh and seventeenth chapters on women and women's education, of President Stanley Hall's *Adolescence.* Michelet's sickening sentimentality and horrible over-sexuality seemed to me to breathe again from every pseudo-scientific page. But how vast the difference between then and now in my feelings, and in the feelings of every woman who has had to do with the education of girls! Then I was terror-struck lest I, and every other woman with me, were doomed to live as pathological invalids in a universe merciless to women as a sex. Now we know that it is not we, but the man who believes such things about us, who is himself pathological, blinded by neurotic mists of sex, unable to see that women form one-half of the kindly race of normal, healthy human creatures in the world; that women, like men, are quickened and inspired by the same study of the great traditions of their race, by the same love of learning, the same love of science, the same love of abstract truth; that women, like men, are immeasurably benefited, physically, mentally and morally, and are made vastly better mothers, as men are made vastly better fathers, by subordinating the distracting instincts of sex to the simple human fellowship of similar education and similar intellectual and social ideals.

It was not to be wondered at that we were uncertain in those old days as to the ultimate result of women's education. Before I myself went to college I had never seen but one college woman. I had heard that such a woman was staying at the house of an acquaintance. I went to see her with fear. Even if she had appeared in hoofs and horns I was determined to go to college all the same. But it was a relief to find this Vassar graduate tall and handsome and dressed like other women. When, five years later, I went to Leipzig to study after I had been graduated from Cornell, my mother used to write me that my name was never mentioned to her by the women of her acquaintance. I was thought by·them to be as much of a disgrace to my family as if I had eloped with the coachman. Now, women who have been to college are as plentiful as blackberries on summer hedges. Even my native city of Baltimore is full of them, and women who have in addition studied in Germany are regarded with becoming deference by the very Baltimore women who disapproved of me.

During the quarter of the century of the existence of the Association of Collegiate Alumnae two generations of college women have reached mature life, and the older generation is now just passing off the stage. We are therefore better prepared than ever before to give an account of what has been definitely accomplished, and to predict what will be the tendencies of women's college and university education in the future.

The curriculum of our women's colleges has steadily stiffened. Women, both in separate, and in coeducational colleges, seem to prefer the old-fashioned, so-called disciplinary studies. They disregard the so-called accomplishments. I believe that to-day more women than men are receiving a thoro college education, even altho in most cases they are receiving it sitting side by side with men in the same college lecture rooms.

The old type of untrained woman teacher has practically disappeared from women's colleges. Her place is being taken by ardent young women scholars who have qualified themselves by long years of graduate study for advanced teaching. Even the old-fashioned untrained matron, or house-mother, is swiftly being replaced in girls' schools, as well as in women's colleges, by the college-bred warden or director.

We did not know when we began whether women's health could stand the strain of college education. We were haunted in those early days by the clanging chains of that gloomy little specter, Dr. Edward H. Clarke's *Sex in education.* With trepidation of spirit I made my mother read it, and was much cheered by her remark that, as neither she, nor any of the women she knew, had ever seen girls or women of the kind described in Dr. Clarke's book, we might as well act as if they did not exist. Still, we did not *know* whether colleges might not produce a crop of just such invalids. Doctors insisted that they would. We women could not be sure until we had tried the experiment. Now we have tried it, and tried it for more than a generation, and we know that college women are not only not invalids, but that they are better physically than other women in their own class of life. We know that girls are growing stronger and more athletic. Girls enter college each year in better physical condition. For the past four years I have myself questioned closely all our entering classes, and often their mothers as well. I find that an average of sixty per cent. enter college absolutely and in every respect well, and that less than thirty per cent. make, or need to make, any periodic difference whatever in exercise, or study, from year's end to year's end. This result is very different from that obtained by physicians and others writing in recent magazines and medical journals. These alarmists give grewsome statistics from high schools and women's colleges, which they are very careful not to name. Probably they are investigating girls whose general hygienic conditions are bad. The brothers of such girls would undoubtedly make as poor a showing physically when compared to Harvard and Yale men, or the boys of Groton or St. Paul's, as their sisters make when compared to Bryn Mawr students. Certainly their sisters who have not been to high school or college would in all probability be even more invalided and abnormal. Seventy per cent. of the Bryn Mawr students come from private schools and from homes where the nutrition and sanitary conditions are excellent. They have undoubtedly been subjected up to the age of nearly nineteen to strenuous and prolonged college preparation, yet their physical condition is far above that of the girls of these other investigations. One investigation yields the shocking result that sixty-six per cent. of college freshmen are practically invalids during certain times in each month, and another that seventy-three per cent. of high school girls are in similar condition. If such results are to be credited, the explanation must be found, as I have said, in the general mal-nutrition and unsanitary life of such girls. Here, as so often when women are investigated, causes which would produce ill-health in boys are not excluded. Surely the Bryn Mawr students approach much more nearly to the normal type. Those other girls are horribly abnormal.

We are now living in the midst of great and, I believe on the whole beneficent, social changes which are preparing the way for the coming economic independence of women. Like the closely allied diminishing birth rate, but unlike the higher education of women, this great

change in opinion and practise seems to have come
about almost without our knowledge, certainly without
our conscious coöperation. The passionate desire of the
women of my generation for a college education seems,
as we study it now in the light of coming events, to have
been a part of this greater movement.

In order to prepare for this economic independence,
we should expect to see what is now taking place. Colleges for women and college departments of coeducational universities are attended by ever-increasing numbers of women students. In seven of the largest western
universities women already outnumber men in the college departments.

A liberal college course prepares women for their
great profession of teaching. College women have proved
to be such admirably efficient teachers that they are driving other women out of the field. Until other means of
self-support are as easy for women as teaching, more
and more women who intend to teach will go to college.
Such women will elect first of all the subjects taught by
women in the high schools, such as Latin, history, and
the languages. They will avoid chemistry, physics, and
other sciences which are usually taught by men. Until
all women become self-supporting, more women than
men will go to college for culture, especially in the west,
and such women will tend to elect the great disciplinary
studies which men neglect because they are intrinsically
more difficult and seem at first sight less practical. For
these obvious reasons certain college courses are therefore already crowded by women and almost deserted by
men in many of the coeducational universities.

And just because women have shown such an aptitude
for a true college education and such delight in it, we
must be careful to maintain it for them in its integrity.

We must see to it that its disciplinary quality is not lowered by the insertion of so-called practical courses which are falsely supposed to prepare for life. Women are rapidly coming to control women's college education. It rests with us to decide whether we shall barter for a mess of pottage the inheritance of the girls of this generation which the girls of my generation agonized to obtain for themselves and for other girls.

We know now that college women marry in about the same proportion, and have about the same number of children as their sisters and cousins who have not been to college. We know also that no one nowadays has more than about two children per marriage—neither college men, nor college women, nor the brothers or sisters of college men and women who have not been to college, nor native white American families, nor American immigrant families in the second generation. This great diminution in the birth rate has taken place notably in the United States, France, Great Britain, and Australia, and is manifesting itself in lesser, but ever increasing degrees, in all other civilized countries. In bringing about this great social change college women have borne no appreciable part. Indeed, only one-half a college woman in every 1000 women is married, the ratio of college women to other women being as 1 to 1000. Although this diminishing birth rate is wholly independent of women's college education, it can not fail to effect it greatly. If it is true, as it seems to be, that college women who marry will have on an average only two children apiece, they could not, if they wished, spend all their time in caring for these two rapidly growing up children, who, moreover, after ten years will be at school, unless they perform also the actual manual labor of their households. In such cases women will presumably prefer to do other work in order to be able to pay wages to have this manual labor done for them. No college-bred man would be willing day after day to shovel coal in his cellar, or to curry and harness his horses, if by more intellectual and interesting labor he could earn enough to pay to have it done for him. Nor will college women be willing to do household drudgery if it can be avoided. Such married women must, therefore, also be prepared for self-support. Likewise the increasingly small proportion of the married fifty per cent. who will marry men able to support them and their two children in comfort will not wish to be idle. They too must be prepared for some form of public service. Of course, the fifty per cent. of college women who do not marry, that is, all except the very few who will inherit fortunes large enough to live on thruout life, must be prepared for self-support.

It seems, therefore, self-evident that practically all women, like practically all men, must look forward after leaving college to some form of public service, whether paid, as it will be for the great majority of both men and women, or unpaid, does not matter. Why should not women, like liberally educated men, fit themselves after college for their special work? When their life-work is more or less determined, let those women who expect to marry and keep their own houses (after all, the women householders will be only about half even of those who marry, say twenty-five per cent. of all college women) study domestic and sanitary science. But it is as unreasonable to compel all women to study it irrespective of their future work as it would be to compel all men to study dentistry or medicine. It is the same with child-study and all other specialized studies.

They belong, one and all, in the graduate professional school.

I believe also that every women's college ought to maintain not only a graduate school of philosophy of the highest grade, but also for holders of the bachelor's degree only a purely graduate school of education connected with a small practise school like the famous practise school of the University of Jena. Only so can we make true and inspired teachers of this vast throng of women going out of our women's colleges into the schoolrooms of the country. The fate of the next generation of children is in their eager hands. It is our mission to see to it that they are as enlightened and as truly wise as they are eager. I know of no way except by teaching them in our graduate schools to reverence abstract truth.

But there is still another and, as it seems to me, more cogent reason for our women's colleges maintaining graduate schools of philosophy. The highest service which colleges can render to their time is to discover and foster imaginative and constructive genius. Such genius unquestionably needs opportunity for its highest development. This is peculiarly the case with women students. As I watch their gallant struggles I sometimes think that the very stars in their courses are conspiring against them. Women scholars can assist women students, as men can not, to tide over the first discouragements of a life of intellectual renunciation. Ability of the kind I am speaking of is, of course, very rare, but for this reason it is precious beyond all other human products. If the graduate schools of women's colleges could develop one single woman of Galton's "X" type—say a Madame Curié, or a Madame Kovalewsky born under a happier star—they would have done more for human advancement than if they had turned out thousands of ordinary college graduates.

The time has now come for those of us who are in control of women's education to bend ourselves to the task of creating academic conditions favorable for the development of this kind of creative ability. We should at once begin to found research chairs for women at all our women's colleges, with three or four hours a week research teaching and the rest of the time free for independent investigation. We should reserve all the traveling fellowships in our gift for women who have given evidence, however slight, of power to do research work. We should bring pressure on our state universities to give such women opportunities to compete for professors' chairs. In the four woman suffrage states this can be accomplished in the twinkling of an eye: it will only be necessary for women's organizations to vote for university regents with proper opinions. The Johns Hopkins University situated in conservative Baltimore has two women on its academic staff who are lecturing to men. Why can not all chairs in the arts departments of universities, that is, in the college and school of philosophy, be thrown open to the competition of women? This is the next advance to be made in women's education—the last and greatest battle to be won.

Only women know how true it is that in the development of the highest scientific and scholarly qualifications women have today far less favorable conditions than even men in Mississippi.

Mr. Havelock Ellis found that in Great Britain women of genius formed only one-twentieth of the whole number. Professor Odin found that in France women of talent were in precisely the same proportion, only one-twentieth of the whole number, but that women furnished 29 per cent. of eminent actors, and 20 per cent. of all prose writers of distinction. In Great Britain likewise 53 per cent. of all women of genius were authors, and 30 per cent. actors. The explanation is clear. Women of genius and talent had more opportunity to come to the surface in these two professions. In all probability the same proportion of women of genius and talent were born with aptitude for scientific research, but were crushed by their unfavorable environment.

It seems to me then to rest with us, the college women of this generation, to see to it that the girls of the next generation are given favorable conditions for this higher kind of scholarly development. To advance the bounds of human knowledge, however little, is to exercise our highest human faculty. There is no more altruistic satisfaction, no purer delight. I am convinced that we can do no more useful work than this—to make it possible for the few women of creative and constructive genius born in any generation to join the few men of genius in their generation in the service of their common race.

16. Marriage and the Woman Scholar[*]

By 1913, President Thomas was ready to trust that the wave of history which had already carried women so far would eventually make possible the combination of marriage and a career. Yet, since she arrived at this hope easily and late, the family never possessed for her the solemnity it had for Catharine Beecher; nor did she dream that it might involve the disordering reality Margaret Fuller had discovered through her child. Rather, she continued to insist that women, like men, found "their greatest happiness in congenial work."

You have asked me, Madam President, to speak to-day of the future of women's college education. You have bid me turn away from the splendid triumphal progress of the past seventy-five years in which Mount Holyoke has blazed the way and led us all and look into the future to discern the path along which she and her sister colleges will travel during the next seventy-five years.

For those of us who are—if I may express the point of view of this platform and say—on the *right* side of fifty, and have spent more than a quarter of a century in educating women it is exhilarating to pause at some such milestone as this anniversary to look forward. We have

[*] M. Carey Thomas, "The Future of Woman's Higher Education," *Mount Holyoke College: The Seventy-fifth Anniversary* (South Hadley, Mass., 1913), pp. 100–104.

gone only a small part of the way but the rest will be easier going. For women's higher education, and indeed the whole woman movement, has been caught in the grip of a great social change and is being carried forward with resistless force.

Much has already been achieved. Women have almost won the right to study what and where they please. They have to-day almost equal opportunities for study. But they have not yet won the rewards of study. They are still shut out from the incentives to scholarship. Over one half of all women college graduates teach, one third of all graduate students in the United States are women fitting themselves for higher teaching. Yet even in the lower public schools the most responsible and highly paid positions are reserved for men and in the few women's colleges only may women compete with men for full professorships. In all coeducational colleges and universities the number of women holding even subordinate teaching positions is jealously limited. Presidents of coeducational universities have sometimes told me that they would gladly advance women scholars were it not for the opposition of men teaching in the same departments. Even in a women's college like Bryn Mawr there is a steady, although I believe almost unconscious, pressure exerted by some of the men on our faculty to prevent the appointment of women to vacant professorships. Men who have taught women at Bryn Mawr (and sometimes only women and never men) for as many as ten or fifteen years will say to me on accepting a call elsewhere: "Of course, my position can only be filled by a man. I do not know why it is but my subject can be best taught by men." This is a natural and inevitable result of women's past. It is not fair to blame men for recognizing it. The life of the intellect and spirit has been lived only by men. The world of scholarship and research has been a man's world. Men mistrust women's ability to breathe in this keener air. And in a sense they are right. Very few women—or men—can maintain scholarly research and enthusiastic teaching throughout a lifetime without living salaries or honourable recognition. Colleges for women few and poorly endowed as they are offer the only rewards for women scholars.

Women scholars have another and still more cruel handicap. They may have spent half a lifetime in fitting themselves for their chosen work and then may be asked to choose between it and marriage. No one can estimate the number of women who remain unmarried in revolt before such a horrible alternative. At Bryn Mawr we have never closed the engagement of a woman professor who wished to marry. Several years ago I persuaded a young woman scholar whose husband was called to Bryn Mawr to take up college teaching again. She told me afterwards that it was like paradise on earth to shut herself into her study in the college library among her books for long hours of intellectual work. How many men scholars would there be if we compelled them to make such an inhuman choice? As a result of this unsocial treatment of women there is a large and ever increasing body of celibate women and men in every civilized country. The best women and many of the best men are unable to marry because of lack of means to found a family. When women can continue their professions and unite their incomes with their husbands' incomes men and women can afford to marry.

The next advance in women's education is then to throw open to the competition of women scholars the rewards and prizes of a scholar's life and to allow women professors like men professors to marry, or not, as they see fit. No one year after year can come in contact with many hundreds of eager young women scholars as I do in our graduate school without feeling sure that equal opportunity will develop many true research workers and productive scholars among women. There seems to me reason to believe that the peculiar qualities of women—patience, dogged persistence, unswerving pursuit of the thing itself, and a certain kind of self-sacrificing idealism may specially fit them for research and higher teaching. In nursing, library work, stenography, type-writing, bookkeeping, and school teaching these and other qualities make it difficult for men to compete with women. We do not yet know what women can do in intellectual and scholarly things. They have done so wonderfully well—really so inconceivably well—against such heavy odds in the past seventy-five years that I venture to predict an altogether astonishing success in the immediate future. For we are now about to take this next step forward.

I have said that women's higher education was only part and parcel of the great social revolution which is now upon us. It is already clear that this transformation of society, of which universal woman suffrage is only a small part, will give equal opportunity to women in every field of human effort including teaching and scholarship. Wherever women vote, which will soon be everywhere in the civilized world, women will be elected equally with men on all school and university boards. Education is women's peculiar public interest. As an immediate consequence women will compete freely with men for all state-supported university professorships. Nor will marriage any longer disqualify women. Women will never deprive other women of a livelihood or of a dearly loved profession because they wish to marry. This has been done in the past only because men do not yet understand that women, like themselves, find their greatest happiness in congenial work.

This great change will affect the future development of colleges for women only favorably. All forms of women's higher education will be needed. We cannot have too many colleges or too many kinds of colleges. In the past women's colleges have given a college education to thousands of girls from conservative homes who otherwise would have had no education. Men professors in women's colleges have dedicated themselves to teaching women with a whole-hearted devotion which they cannot give in coeducational colleges where men students are necessarily their chief interest. Professorships in Mount Holyoke and Wellesley and in many smaller women's colleges have in the past been filled only by women. These communities of women scholars have advanced the cause of women's education out of all proportion to their numbers because they have been, as it were, set on a hill in women's colleges. Vassar and Smith and Bryn Mawr have proved that eminent men and women scholars can work together in college departments. At Bryn Mawr women are as often heads of departments as men. Bryn Mawr has shown that graduate work and Ph.D. degrees given by a woman's college can hold their own against the competition of co-educational universities. Women's colleges have made distinct contributions to higher education. They have maintained on the whole higher standards of academic work than men's colleges. They have proved that it is possible to make a whole student body work hard and like to work hard. They seem to me to have solved the problems of college athletics by forbidding all intercollegiate games. They are now about to deal with secret societies. They have steadily insisted on a four years' college course of liberal culture. As in the past so for the indefinite future women's colleges will continue to fill a great need.

Indeed, women's colleges have accomplished so much with such meagre resources that I often wonder how wealthy men and women can resist the temptation of endowing them liberally. Women are the teachers of the race. Women are the mothers of its children, The problems of women which are the problems of the world must be solved in great part in colleges for women. A few million dollars apiece, or even one million dollars apiece, given to Mount Holyoke and her sister women's colleges, would bear fruit an hundredfold in human welfare and human happiness.

BARBARA M. CROSS, Assistant Professor of English at Barnard College, was born in Pittsfield, Massachusetts, in 1924. She received her B.A. from Smith College, her M.A. from Yale University, and her Ph.D. from Radcliffe College. Professor Cross taught English at Bryn Mawr College from 1952 until 1958. Her publications include *Horace Bushnell: Minister to a Changing America* (1958) and *The Autobiography of Lyman Beecher* (edited, 1961).